STAND STRONG IN YOUR FAITH

LIVE WHAT YOU BELIEVE WITH CONFIDENCE AND PASSION

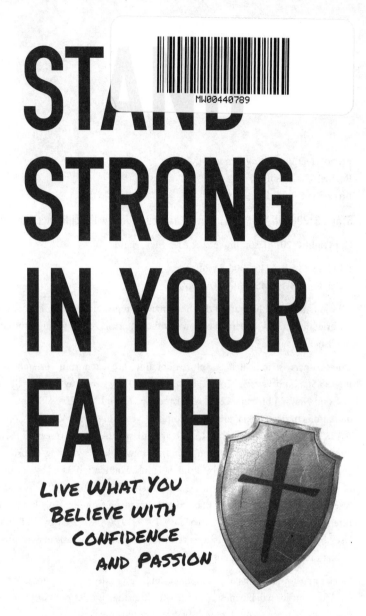

Jason Jimenez • Alex McFarland

BroadStreet Publishing Group, LLC
Racine, Wisconsin, USA
BroadStreetPublishing.com

STAND STRONG IN YOUR FAITH: Live What You Believe with Confidence and Passion

ISBN-13: 978-1-4245-5306-8 (softcover)
ISBN-13: 978-1-4245-5307-5 (e-book)

Stock or custom editions of BroadStreet Publishing titles may be purchased in bulk for educational, business, ministry, fundraising, or sales promotional use. For information, please e-mail info@broadstreetpublishing.com.

Cover design: Chris Garborg /garborgdesign.com
Interior design and typeset: Katherine Lloyd/theDESKonline.com

Printed in the United States of America

17 18 19 20 21 5 4 3 2 1

CONTENTS

A Faith Workout... 5

Chapter 1   When in Doubt... 9

Chapter 2   How to Be Fearless in the Midst of Fear........................ 23

Chapter 3   Living Beyond Yourself: The Role of the Holy Spirit in a Believer's Life... 37

Chapter 4   The Most Neglected Thing in America: The Bible.................. 51

Chapter 5   How Can I Know the Bible Is True? 67

Chapter 6   The Crux of History: Did Jesus Rise from the Dead?................ 83

Chapter 7   What's the Best Way to Study the Bible? 107

Chapter 8   Six Christian Duties to Keep You Strong........................119

Notes   133

About the Authors..139

A FAITH WORKOUT

The common response when someone asks you how you're doing is to say, "I'm good." But what would you say if someone asked you about how your faith was doing? Would you say it's good? Would you say it is strong? Or weak? Or maybe even nonexistent?

What we have found in our combined forty years of ministry is that most Christians have a defeated faith. Throughout the Bible we are told to "be courageous" and to "stand strong in your faith." And yet there are many Christians today who are throwing in the towel and giving up altogether. We think this is a shame and unnecessary.

That's why we felt compelled to write this book. We want to help you not only stand strong in your faith but also do so with great passion and conviction as you impact the lives of those around you. If you feel your faith is not as strong as you would like it to be, know that we are glad you have picked up this book. We are thrilled at the opportunity to take you on this faith workout. Think of this time together like hitting the gym. Before you freak out and toss the book aside—please, hear us out.

As Christians, our entire lives are built on the foundation of faith. Every human being expresses and exercises some form of faith. Yet, for the most part, Christians duck and cover rather than exercise their faith. They'd much rather sit in the pews, watching and hearing from their fellow believers who are working out their faith, rather than work out their own faith. That's the easy thing to do. But do you *really* want that for yourself? Don't you want to have a strong faith that can make a supernatural difference in your life and in the lives of those around you?

We want to help motivate Christians to hit the "faith gym" and start building up their spiritual muscles. The world desperately needs stronger Christians who can step up, motivate, and inspire a whole new generation to stand strong in their faith. But this won't happen if Christians have a weak and untrained faith.

It takes a commitment to build up your faith. It will take discipline and hard work. But we believe you can do it with the help of the Holy Spirit and by spending time in God's Word. Much like physical training, you will have good spiritual workouts and not-so-good ones. There will be times when you will have to dig deep to maximize the most of your faith and pull through. But don't worry; we are here to train alongside of you. Look to us as your spiritual coaches.

In *Stand Strong in Your Faith*, we walk through some of the most common areas that prevent Christians from having a strong and robust faith. It is our goal to change that. In this book, you will come face-to-face with your fears and doubts, and learn to deal with them according to the Word of God. We will also train you on how to walk in the Holy Spirit, and thus you will gain invaluable insights into how to pray with power, share your faith, and persevere in the midst of hard times.

Are you ready to start strengthening your faith? Then let's hit the faith gym.

Jason Jimenez & Alex McFarland
Spring of 2017

Be on your guard; stand strong in the faith.
—1 CORINTHIANS 16:13

CHAPTER 1

WHEN IN DOUBT

*Feed your faith and your doubts
will starve to death.*

—UNKNOWN

Have you ever doubted what you believe as a Christian? If so, know that you're not alone. Doubt is a normal struggle in the faith. Every Christian (including your pastor) has had doubts. Would it surprise you to know that legends like John the Baptist, John Calvin, C. S. Lewis, Charles Spurgeon, and Martin Luther all struggled with deep doubts?

We have had our fair share of doubts in our walk with Christ too. We've questioned the reliability of the Bible, doubted our salvation, and have even felt that prayer was a waste of time. But whenever we were at that halfway point—between belief and disbelief—we had to ask some questions: What's causing my doubt? What does God's Word say about doubt? How can I prevent doubt from consuming my life? Asking these questions is a deliberate process. It forces one to address the doubt, figure out how it happened, and decide on the appropriate steps necessary to rectify those doubts.

Unfortunately, this is not something Christians know how to do well. Talking about doubt makes us uneasy. We feel judged. Or we feel a sense of shame for calling into question God's love for us. Some can get so overwhelmed by doubt that it stirs up more worry and doubt. This is the crazy cycle of doubt. And the longer a Christian rides this crazy cycle, the more ineffective he or she will be for God.

But would it surprise you to know that the Bible includes many examples of doubt? For example, did you know that Abraham doubted God? He even laughed (or mocked) God's promise that he would have a son in his old age. What about Moses? Or doubting Thomas (as we like to call him)? Did not these men doubt at one time or another in their lives? They did. But the thing is that their doubts didn't lead them to unbelief. Rather, their doubts led them to a greater journey of faith.

These stories are recorded in the Bible to help us overcome doubt in each of our lives. No matter if the doubt is big or small, the Word of God is the answer to defeating any kind of doubt we may have. Despite the trouble you might be facing with doubt, understand that God is faithful and He has given you the Spirit of truth to help you walk and grow in a true and lasting relationship with Him.

However, every Christian must be aware that satan uses doubt as a mechanism to destroy his or her communion with God and flood that individual with concerns. He will target your boldness and keep the attacks coming until you break. Satan wants to strip away any certainty you have in God and replace it with uncertainty. That's his goal.

But we (Jason and Alex) want you to know that our prayer is that you won't allow satan to use doubt as a ploy to break your intimacy with God. Our goal, especially in this chapter, is to embolden you to not let doubt go unchecked in your life. We want to help you properly address your concerns, questions, and doubts—and, Lord willing, bring you the necessary remedy to soothe your wandering soul.

DOUBTS ABOUT MY FAITH

Does God really love me?
Can I trust the Bible?
Can I lose my salvation?
Does my church even care?
How can I be sure what I believe is true?
Did Jesus really rise from the dead?
What if all this isn't real?

Entertaining Doubts

In the church, and even beyond the doors of the church, are millions of Christians who are consumed with doubts. I (Jason) was speaking at Summit Ministries[1] one summer and remember having a lot of conversations with millennials about their doubts. One student told me that he tried discussing his doubts about his faith with his pastor but felt judged. Another student told me she doubted that God had truly forgiven her of her sexual past.

After speaking at a church in Texas, we (Jason and Alex) had a couple who approached us after the event. They were visibly distraught. After some small talk, we asked them how we could help. They shared about their marriage troubles and how they were seeking counsel on a few issues. This couple was consumed with doubt. In fact, there wasn't anything they didn't doubt. They doubted their marriage, they doubted their faith, they doubted their parenting, and they doubted the leadership at their church. After listening to them for a bit, we asked them one simple question: "Do you pray?" The husband looked at his wife, and then looked over at us again and said, "I don't have the faith to pray anymore."

These people represent just a fraction of the doubt that is plaguing Christians today. We are living in a day when there are a lot of doubters. And the last place one would think to find them would be at church. But the church is filled with doubters— doubters who have neglected to confront their doubts, and, as a result, are becoming more skeptical in their faith. They may not reject Jesus as Savior, but they are living a dejected faith that is leading them farther down a path of doubt, worry, anxiety, and frustration.

But as we mentioned before, doubting is a normal process. The truth is that we are going to doubt. We are not perfect. We will have our issues with God and raise questions about life that will (from time to time) go unanswered. That's life. Doubts will cause us to hit rock bottom, but as long as our faith is built on the Rock, then we will be just fine.

> Doubts will cause us to hit rock bottom, but as long as our faith is
> built on the Rock, then we will be just fine.

Author and pastor Timothy Keller sheds some light on the tension between faith and doubt in every Christian's life:

> A faith without some doubts is like a human body without
> any antibodies in it. People who blithely go through life
> too busy or indifferent to ask hard questions about why

they believe as they do will find themselves defenseless against either the experience of tragedy or the probing questions of a smart skeptic. A person's faith can collapse almost overnight if she has failed over the years to listen patiently to her own doubts, which should only be discarded after long reflection.[2]

Thus it's important that we understand the role of doubt in each of our lives—not only from our human perspective but for God's sake as well. Let's now look at the different kinds of doubt and see what we can learn about each type.

The Three Kinds of Doubt

Doubt comes in all shapes and sizes. But before we delineate the different forms of doubt, we want to share with you some insight from an expert who also happens to be a friend of ours. His name is Dr. Gary Habermas, and he wrote a fantastic book called *Dealing with Doubt*. In this book, Habermas writes:

> The fact that human beings are whole, rather than being fragmented into their component "parts" is a reminder that uncertainty generally affects the entire person. As a result, causes of doubt are seldom individual but are interrelated with each other. Attempting to unravel the moral, social, medical and psychological factors for purposes of identification can indeed be troublesome.[3]

Habermas makes an important point: Getting to the core of doubt takes considerable effort. There are so many variables and interrelated pieces. It's one thing to recognize doubt in your life but quite another to identify its root cause. I (Jason) remember talking with a young woman about her doubts. She knew exactly what her doubts were but couldn't figure out why they were there. The more she tried to solve the cause of her doubts, the more stressed she felt.

To help further understand doubt and provide a clearer way to distinguish the different kinds of doubt, we are going to use Habermas' three groupings of doubt as a preliminary step to find healing. The three most common aspects of doubt are emotional doubt, reasonable doubt, and volitional doubt.

Emotional Doubt

Emotional doubt is the worst kind of doubt. It is also the most painful. Emotional doubt has more to do with feelings than facts and frequently involves a person's subjective responses, not objective reality. People with emotional doubt are typically those who have experienced a tragedy in their life. The death of a loved one, a bad breakup, a loss of a job, or anything that brings with it emotional and physical pain can cause emotional doubt. Anxiety and depression are also common causes of emotional doubt and can lead down a path of unspeakable damage. Habermas said this about emotional doubt:

> Emotional doubt frequently poses as its factual sister. It has some of the same concerns and raises some of the same questions. Yet, the issues are determined and the evidence is judged by how one feels about them. Conclusions come from one's moods or feelings. The emotional doubter is often very intelligent and appears to be raising serious objections to the truthfulness of Christianity. But, in reality, the uncertainty is not primarily factual and the questions are far more subjective.[4]

Another thing to realize about emotional doubt is that it is often stirred up by demonic activity. In his classic book *The Screwtape Letters*, C. S. Lewis fancifully articulates the pressure of doubt brought on by demons:

> But you can worry him with the haunting suspicion that the practice is absurd and can have no objective result. Don't forget to use the "Heads I win, tails you lose" argument. If the thing he prays for doesn't happen, then that is one more proof that petitionary prayers don't work; if it does happen, he will, of course, be able to see some of the physical causes which led up to it, and "therefore it would have happened anyway," and thus a granted prayer becomes just as good a proof as a denied one that prayers are ineffective.[5]

Reasonable (Factual) Doubt

Reasonable doubt is mainly concerned with the evidential foundation of belief. It's brought on when a certain belief is challenged with a new set of information. This form of doubt is not to be confused with skepticism. It's one thing to be skeptical about a new challenge or new piece of information, but it's quite another to question everything and never come to grips with the facts (no matter what they are). This is not the case with *reason*able doubt (hence the term).

Someone with reasonable doubts doesn't believe just because someone says she is supposed to believe. If something doesn't make sense (if there is an apparent contradiction) to her, she will investigate until she gets the answers for which she is looking. And she won't let it go until she gets answers. For the most part, reasonable doubt is motivated by a lack of credible answers. Just like in the court of law, if the jurors cannot conclude "beyond a reasonable doubt" that the defendant is guilty, then they must acquit. Likewise, to have reasonable doubt is to admit a level of uncertainty.

Volitional Doubt

Volitional doubt exists solely because the person is *unwilling* to believe. No matter how overwhelming the facts or evidence is, it doesn't matter to him. In the case of an unbeliever, he deliberately rejects the truth of God. He doesn't want to admit his need for God. He wants to live for himself. This is kind of like the Huxley brothers, Thomas and Aldous. They didn't want to be under moral restraints; they wanted sexual freedom. Therefore, no matter how convincing Christianity was to them, they willfully chose to reject it.

Remember Bertrand Russell? He was one of the greatest philosophers, skeptics, and atheists of his time. This question was posed to him: "If you were to stand before the Lord, what would you say?" Russell arrogantly replied, "You did not provide me enough evidence." Talk about a rebellious heart. But this is exactly what happens when a person chooses to harden his or her heart to the truth.

On the other hand, in the case of a believer, she can also harden her heart toward God. But does this mean she is rejecting Christ as her Lord and Savior? No. What we mean is that a Christian (who volitionally doubts) is freely choosing not to trust in God. This ranges from an undeveloped (weak) form of faith to a lack of motivation to follow the Word of God and thus choosing to sin despite the consequences. This is the most dangerous of doubts because the Christian is volitionally choosing to turn from God.

The more a Christian gives in to his or her own sinful desires, the less care and devotion he or she will have toward the things of God. Paul warns in 1 Thessalonians 5:19 that we are not to "quench the Spirit." For Paul to give this warning, it is implied that we can disregard (or willfully refuse) the conviction of the Holy Spirit. The only remedy for volitional doubt is repentance (to change our attitude toward God).

Overcoming Doubt

We are now going to offer biblical and practical ways to address and deal with each form of doubt. It's important to mention that we all struggle with each form of doubt (emotional, reasonable, and volitional) in our lives. However, there is always that one form of doubt that we will be more sensitive to than others. We need to be aware of this, because it will help us isolate and explain (to some degree) why we're struggling with doubt in the first place.

Dealing with Emotional Doubt

C. S. Lewis so fittingly reminds us that our faith will go through seasons of drought and doubt. He writes, "Faith, in the sense in which I am here using the word, is the art of holding on to things your reason has once accepted, in spite of your changing moods. … That is why Faith is such a necessary virtue: unless you teach your moods 'where they get off,' you can never be either a sound Christian or even a sound atheist."[6]

The challenge here is whether you let the truth of God rule your life or whether you give in to the fears of the flesh. Emotional doubters fixate on what-ifs all the time. However, faith doesn't thrive on moods. Faith thrives when it holds fast to the Word of God. In 2 Peter 1:5–9, we are told how to grow in our faith:

Make every effort to add to your faith goodness; and to goodness, knowledge; and to knowledge, self-control; and to self-control, perseverance; and to perseverance, godliness; and to godliness, mutual affection; and to mutual affection, love. For if you possess these qualities in increasing measure, they will keep you from being ineffective and unproductive in your knowledge of our Lord Jesus Christ. But whoever does not have them is nearsighted and blind, forgetting that they have been cleansed from their past sins. (NIV)

Os Guinness states it this way: "What is more, faith, like health, is best maintained by growth, nourishment and exercise and not by fighting sickness. ... Equally, faith grows and flourishes when it is well nourished and exercised, so the best way to resist doubt is to build up faith rather than simply to fight against doubt."[7]

The more you seek to be filled with the Holy Spirit and devote your life to faithful prayer, the less likely your life will be filled with emotional doubts. Often, we can let emotional doubt creep in when we allow uncertainty or ignorance of God's Word to control our actions. When we start to feel this, the last thing we want to do is make decisions based on how we feel. That is not wise. To gain wisdom, James 1:5–6, says, "If any of you lacks wisdom, let him ask God, who gives generously to all without reproach, and it will be given him. But let him ask *in faith, with no doubting,* for the one who doubts is like a wave of the sea that is driven and tossed by the wind."

Perhaps you doubt because you have a misconstrued under-standing of God. Or maybe you doubt because you underwent a traumatic experience and have never recovered from it. Or per-haps you struggle with abandonment issues, which is what causes you to doubt. Whatever the reason, until you truly give this over to God, you will always battle with this form of doubt.

Therefore, *the key is to not give into your feelings but to exercise faith in God.* Emotions change, but God never changes. Emotions can lie to you, but God never lies. These are some truths you can hold on to as you seek to overcome emotional doubt in your life.

Dealing with Reasonable Doubt

If someone says, "This isn't making sense," or, "I'm having a hard time believing …" or "Yeah, but what do you do with …" it doesn't mean they're a skeptic. Rather, they may be asking legitimate questions because they're legitimately seeking reasonable answers. A true skeptic is not someone who never believes, but someone who is open to believe but vigorously questions until he or she is satisfied.

The cool thing is that the Bible welcomes this kind of doubt. First John 5:13 says, "I write these things to you who believe in the name of the Son of God so that you may know that you have eternal life" (NIV). Elsewhere, Paul writes to the Thessalonians, "Test everything; hold fast what is good" (1 Thessalonians 5:21).

Remember the disciple Thomas? You know, the guy we refer to as doubting Thomas? In John 20, we read that the disciples told Thomas that they had seen the resurrected Christ (see v. 25). Thomas responds by saying, "Unless I see in his hands the mark of the nails, and place my finger into the mark of the nails, and place my hand into his side, I will never believe" (v. 25). This is why people have come to know him as "doubting Thomas." However, we don't see it that way. We think Thomas has gotten a bad rap.

Thomas, no doubt (pun intended), was under duress (like the rest of the disciples). Their Master had just been brutally murdered, and they feared the Romans were coming to capture them. They all had reason to doubt. So when the disciples, amid all the chaos, told Thomas (who hadn't been with them at the time) that they witnessed the risen Christ, they were expecting him to believe them. But to believe, Thomas needed more proof. This meant that he needed to see the resurrected Christ. He needed to see (for himself) the body that carried the scars of the crucifixion. That's not unreasonable. Thomas put forward some reasonable criteria if he was to believe. Notice that Thomas took what he knew to be true about the crucifixion (facts), and then specified what further evidence he would need (in line with the facts) that would persuade him to believe.

The necessary approach is to treat reasonable doubts with reasonable answers. If you fall into this category, then you understand that "neat" or "simplistic" answers aren't what you're looking for. You tend to want to go deeper and treasure more in-depth conversations. There is nothing wrong with this. As a matter of fact, we challenge Christians to engage more in debate with others around them, but to do so with grace and truth (see Colossians 4:6). This can be achieved by seeking out a few mature Christians who are critical thinkers and strong in their faith. These mentor Christians will be a great source to help you when you're investigating, inquiring, and questioning your faith. The key is to further study the tenets of the Christian faith and continue to sharpen your knowledge and skills in apologetics (a reasoned defense of the Christian faith), theology (a reasoned and biblical explanation of Christian teaching), and philosophy (a reasoned approach to any subject, including how to think and analyze).

Dealing with Volitional Doubt

Volitional doubt is often disguised as intellectual in nature. But beneath the questioning and challenging is a person whose heart is hard toward God. For a Christian to reach this point, he has had to have faced many challenges that have made him bitter and afraid. At some point in life, a volitional doubter has given himself over to sin. James makes it clear when he writes, "But each person is tempted when he is lured and enticed by his own desire. Then desire when it has conceived gives birth to sin, and sin when it is fully grown brings forth death" (1:14–15 NIV).

Therefore, the key to overcoming volitional doubt is to repent of your willful disobedience and turn your life back to Christ. A great example of this is found in 2 Corinthians 7. The Corinthians had turned away from Christ because they weren't willing to give up their sexual sin. But after much persuasion by Paul, and much prayer, the Corinthians responded in brokenness and turned back to Christ.

God Will Keep You from Stumbling

There is so much more to be said about doubt, but hopefully you've come away with a few pointers on how to deal with doubt in your life. Mainly, we hope that you don't ignore or disregard the doubts that come up. Every time Jesus spotted weak faith, what did He do? He rebuked it (see Matthew 8:26; 14:31; 16:8). Why? Because weak faith is a sign of strong doubt. It may not always be fatal, but doubt is never trivial.

> A sign of strong faith is one that overcomes doubt, not the other way around.

We pray that you will take your doubts more seriously and rebuke them from your life before they threaten your faith. A sign of strong faith is one that overcomes doubt, not the other way around. Jude prayed for his readers:

Now to him who is able to keep you from stumbling and to present you blameless before the presence of his glory with great joy, to the only God, our Savior, through Jesus Christ our Lord, be glory, majesty, dominion, and authority, before all time and now and forever. Amen. (Jude 24–25)

CHAPTER 2

HOW TO BE FEARLESS IN THE MIDST OF FEAR

Our greatest fear should not be of failure, but of succeeding at something that doesn't really matter.
—D. L. MOODY

D o you think God wants His people living in fear? No, He doesn't. Yet fear exists in all of us. And no matter where we turn, it seems like fear is right around the corner, ready to scare us.

A person can go on phobialist.com and check out all the phobias people have about all sorts of things. There is, of course, arachnophobia (the fear of spiders), acrophobia (the fear of heights), and achluophobia (the fear of darkness), which are some of the most common types of phobias. But did you know there's ambulophobia (the fear of walking) and catoptrophobia (the fear of mirrors), and, get this, there's even a phobia of beautiful women (called caligynephobia). We're just glad you don't have bibliophobia (the fear of books).

The point is that we are all scared of something. When I

(Jason) was a child, I'd get scared if the closet door was left open at night. I'd imagine the bogeyman coming out of that small, dark closet, ready to kill me (or one of my big brothers pulling a prank on me). As a father who is now raising four children, it's interesting to see the various kinds of fears my kids have in different stages of their lives. As I write this, my five-year-old, Hailey, is afraid of the dark. She wants the night-light switched on and the door left open, whereas before she didn't really care.

Growing up, I (Alex) was an introvert. I was terrified of the teacher calling on me to speak or come up in front of the class. In fact, when I was in high school, I was in an English class and almost failed English because I could not get up in front of the class and give a book report. But who would have known that someday I would be an evangelist, speaking in front of thousands of people every year? Talk about overcoming fear. I went from being an extreme introvert to being able to talk to people because Jesus changed my life.

But what about fears that affect us as adults? You know, the kind of fear that prevents us from trusting in God? In this chapter, we're going to talk about the power of fear and the spiritual measures a person can take to prevent fear from crippling him or her. The Bible has a lot to say about fear, so get prepared to learn how to be fearless in the midst of fear.

Sleepless Nights

Back in 1943, the famed artist Norman Rockwell painted a series of paintings called The Four Freedoms. The first of the four paintings, *Freedom of Speech*, is a scene of a man standing to speak at a local town meeting. The second painting, *Freedom of Worship*, beautifully captures the faces of Americans praying. The third painting, *Freedom from Want*, depicts a group of people gathered around the Thanksgiving table. And the fourth and final painting, *Freedom of Fear*, is a powerful picture of a mom and a dad tucking their children into bed, while the dad holds a newspaper detailing the perils of World War II.

Shortly after this period in America, world evangelist Billy Graham said, "Historians will probably call our era 'the age of anxiety.' Anxiety is the natural result when our hopes are centered in anything short of God and His will for us."[1] Billy said this over sixty years ago. If Americans were filled with so much anxiety back then, how much more frightened have we become as a nation today?

Think about the perils we currently face. We fear terrorist attacks. We fear the government is spying on us. We fear the growing corruption of our government and all the corporate tracking of personal information, identity theft, credit card fraud, and the advancement of cyberterrorism. Fearing all of this can drive a person mad. So what do we do about it?

We need to trust in God as our shield, just like when He told Abraham not to fear, but to trust in His protection (see Genesis 15:1). We need to acknowledge that no matter where we go in life, God is our shield. He is our protector. David pronounced, "The LORD is my light and my salvation; whom shall I fear? The LORD is the stronghold of my life; of whom shall I be afraid?" (Psalm 27:1). Notice how intimately David felt about God's protection and the peace and joy he felt because of that protection. This kind of assurance requires time with God. It takes a willingness to trust and obey—even when it's hard (and *especially* when it's hard).

David knew the challenges and threats that faced him (see Psalm 27:2–3), yet despite the vicious attacks and the enemies who encamped around him, he didn't go into panic mode. The main reason is because his focus was not on the earthly threats, but on the beauty and splendor of God. David declared:

> One thing have I asked of the LORD,
>   that will I seek after:
> that I may dwell in the house of the LORD
>   all the days of my life,
> to gaze upon the beauty of the LORD
>   and to inquire in his temple.
> For he will hide me in his shelter
>   in the day of trouble;
> he will conceal me under the cover of his tent;
>   he will lift me high upon a rock. (Psalm 27:4–5)

Here's a great takeaway from David's prayer in Psalm 27: not living a life of fear has more to do with dwelling in the safety of God than it does trying to avoid what scares you.

It's easy to admire and want to emulate David's faith. And we should. I (Jason) have always looked to David as an example of faith. His boldness, leadership, and intimate prayers have been a great inspiration to me. But what made David's faith so great? Was it because he was such an amazing warrior and king? No. Not at all. David's faith was not great because he was king; his faith was great because he placed his trust in the King of kings.

That's the ticket.

> Christians often become focused on how small their faith is, yet the Bible tells us not to focus too much on the size of our faith, but rather on the object of our faith.

Christians often become focused on how small their faith is, yet the Bible tells us not to focus too much on the size of our faith, but rather on the object of our faith. If we overlook the source of our faith, then we can't expect to have much of a faith at all. Our faith is only as strong as its object. Burk Parsons, the editor at *Tabletalk* magazine, sums it up this way:

> Our Father is the source of our assurance, Christ is the ground of our assurance, and the Spirit is the sustainer of our assurance. And our assurance is not established on the strength of our faith but on the object of our faith, Jesus Christ. Therefore, when we doubt, let us remember that when Abraham counted the stars, he was counting you, me, and all those chosen in Christ before the foundation of the world.[2]

As Christians, we have a total guarantee that our faith is secure because its object is Jesus Christ. We have no reason to doubt or fear.

Fear to Fail

We (Jason and Alex) have never met a person who loves to fail. The idea of failure freaks people out. It doesn't matter who you are or what you do—everybody is scared to fail. But the good news is that God's pathway to victory isn't as hard as one may think. God doesn't expect us to do it alone. It is Jesus, the great deliverer, who will give us the boldness to overcome all our fears.

I (Alex) can attest to a time in my life when I was afraid to fail. I was afraid to step out in faith and start a brand-new ministry. I had been a student pastor for seven years and really enjoyed what

I did. I didn't want to leave the comforts of my job at church. I had a secure position that paid the bills. Yet despite my comfort and the fear I felt, I knew God was calling me to start an evangelistic ministry (that ultimately would lead to television and radio). I had a clear vision, but there was a part of me that kept saying, "Yeah, but you're going to be broke in six months. You're going to lose your house, and then what?"

This went on for some time. Every time I pondered the move, my stomach would tighten and I'd tell myself, "You're crazy for thinking this, Alex." Yet here's the thing. One day it was like the Holy Spirit spoke to my heart and said, "Look, you're going to have to believe what's true rather than believe a lie."

The whole time I was believing a lie that brought great fear into my life. Rather than trust in a God who is able, I preferred to rely on my own weakness. God had to remind me of who He is—that He is the Creator of the heavens and the earth. Psalm 147:5 affirms, "Great is our Lord, and abundant in power; his understanding is beyond measure."

But here's the problem: As strong as my belief was in God being all-powerful, why was I still letting fear control my life? If I truly believed that Jesus Christ rose from the grave, then why was I having such a hard time believing Jesus could pay my bills? The moment I acknowledged God's power over my life, it was like the fear disappeared. I was no longer scared to step out in faith and start my evangelistic ministry. I wanted nothing more than to live a life of faith, not one of fear.

What about you? Are you too afraid to do something God has called you to do? Have you been holding onto a dream but too afraid to sow seeds into it because it appears risky? We can't tell you how many dead dreams exist among the older population. Some of the saddest stories we hear come from people in their sixties and seventies. Looking back, many of them wish they took greater risks instead of holding on to their fears. They would give anything to do it all over again. The haunting thoughts of what could have been plaguing them, leaving them to spend the rest of their lives wishing they had listened to God. Do you want to end up like these older folks? Do you want to go through life wishing for what could have been?

> The truth is that fear has killed more dreams than failures. You will never know what could be if you're not willing to find out. And you won't find out if you never face the risk of failure.

There came a point in my (Jason's) life that if I hadn't overcome my fear and left Tucson, Arizona, I would have never become an author. This means that I wouldn't be writing this book. Not only that, I would have never been personally trained and mentored by Dr. Norman Geisler. If I had stayed in Tucson, I would have never met all the people who have helped me launch Stand Strong Ministries. The bottom line is that if I had stayed in Tucson, I wouldn't just be experiencing regret, I'd be living a life of disobedience to God.

Trust me when I say that I had many sleepless nights before my wife and I finally decided to move across the country. There were times we thought we made the wrong decision. But thankfully, we didn't entertain our fears but kept our eyes on Jesus.

Fear is difficult. It's challenging. It's defeating. And, if you let it, fear can lead to disastrous outcomes. That's why there are more inactive Christians living in fear than there are active Christians living fearlessly for Christ. Think about all the times you were too afraid to speak up and share the gospel with someone at work, or too afraid to confront a situation in a relationship. Or what about starting that business, or applying for that job—how many times has the thought, "Yeah, but what if I fail?" crossed your mind?

> But when I am afraid,
> I put my trust in you.
> I praise God for what he has promised.
> I trust in God, so why should I be afraid?
> What can mere mortals do to me?
> —Psalm 56:3–4 NLT

If your life has been consumed by thoughts of fear and doubt, then put your trust in 2 Corinthians 10:4–6: "For the weapons of our warfare are not of the flesh but have divine power to destroy strongholds. We destroy arguments and every lofty opinion raised against the knowledge of God, and take every thought captive to obey Christ, being ready to punish every disobedience, when your obedience is complete."

Ask yourself, "Am I going to let fear or faith determine my future?" Our adequacy to live fearlessly comes from Christ's sufficiency. Second Corinthians 3:5 says, "Not that we are sufficient in ourselves to claim anything as coming from us, but our sufficiency is from God." As you move forward, take hold of this truth: "For God has not given us a spirit of fear and timidity, but of power, love, and self-discipline" (2 Timothy 1:7 NLT). If you're consumed by fear, that is not of God.

Will God Provide?

There are millions of people who worry if God will take care of their needs. I (Jason) live in Charlotte, North Carolina. It's a banking town, which means there's a lot of wealth to go around. Many of the churches are big and pricey. Yet despite the exceeding wealth, people still seem to worry and fret over money. No matter how good we have it, there never seems to be enough.

When I (Alex) was a kid, my mom and dad had severe financial problems. My dad had let the mortgage get behind, and so my parents ended up several hundreds of thousands of dollars in debt. When I was about ten years old, the bank came to put us out of our house. I remember my mother crying. We were all on the front porch of our house watching as my dad pleaded with the banker for more time. The banker wouldn't have it. He told my dad he was out of time and that we needed to leave our house. By God's grace, my dad's friend fronted him some money, and we were able to get our house back.

Because of this traumatic experience as a child, I would have a recurring fear (as an adult) that at any moment my wife and I were going to get evicted from our house, that we were going to be homeless. For the first two decades of our marriage, I was obsessively fearful that at any minute the bank was going to show up and put us out of our house. Of course, this was an irrational fear. I had no reason to believe this would happen. Yet I still did. Troubled by this, I remember talking with a few well-respected leaders. One of the men (a dear friend and pastor), told me I had been obsessing so long over this because of the traumatic fear I experienced when my dad lost our house.

False
Evidence
Appearing
Real

What great insight. My wife and I knew God was taking care of us and that we were relying on Him every day of our lives—except for in this area of my life. And so I took this irrational fear of being homeless and cried out, "Jesus, I'm laying this at the cross. I'm asking you to deliver me from this fear. I pray that it will no longer haunt me. Remove it from my life."

And you know what? He did. I was carrying around a concealed weight of worry and fear for far too long. But thankfully, God had placed godly people in my life to help me deal with the problem. Dr. Gary Collins writes:

> According to the Bible, there is nothing wrong with realistically acknowledging and trying to deal with the identifiable problems of life. To ignore danger is foolish and wrong. But it is also wrong, as well as unhealthy, to be immobilized by excessive worry. Such worry must be committed to prayer to God, who can release us from paralyzing fear or anxiety, and free us to deal realistically with the needs and welfare both of others and of ourselves.[3]

Do you fixate on what you fear you will lack tomorrow? Do you find yourself worrying all the time about how God will provide for your needs? If so, then read what Jesus had to say about worry:

> Therefore do not be anxious, saying, "What shall we eat?" or "What shall we drink?" or "What shall we wear?" For the Gentiles seek after all these things, and your heavenly Father knows that you need them all. But seek first the kingdom of God and his righteousness, and all these things will be added to you.

Therefore do not be anxious about tomorrow, for tomorrow will be anxious for itself. Sufficient for the day is its own trouble. (Matthew 6:31–34)

According to Jesus, it is foolish to worry about the things of this world. Yet what do we do? We worry. We worry about paying the bills. We worry about getting that raise. We worry about how we're going to pay for school. We worry about debt. We worry about how we're going to be able to afford the family vacation. However, Jesus clearly said that our heavenly Father knows what we need better than we do. And like any good parent, the Lord isn't going to neglect meeting our needs. God promises daily bread, not daily wants. Psalm 84:11 states, "The LORD will withhold no good thing from those who do what is right" (NLT).

I (Jason) confess that I am a worrier. As far back as I can remember, I've worried about something. It didn't matter what it was. Will I wake up in time for school? Did I study enough for the test? Will I make the team? Is my dad going to lose his job? My life was consumed with worry. And then, in July 1994, my mom was tragically killed in a car accident. Just like that. She was gone. I remember two weeks prior to my mother's death wondering, *What would I do if my mom died?* Just thinking about that made me worry. I couldn't imagine life without her. Then she was gone.

I'm here to tell you that it was in the hardest times (missing my mom) that God showed up in the most powerful ways. There were rough patches, to be sure. I'd worry and battle with thoughts of fear and doubt, but I kept holding fast to the promises of God. I learned to give my worries to Him (see 1 Peter 5:7).

No matter what you are fretting over or worrying about, you too need to give your worries to God. When you worry about the budget or how you're going to pay the bills, you are letting the things of this world (uncertainty) cloud your judgment. Trust that God is looking out for you. Have faith that God will provide for your daily needs. And as you face uncertainty, remind yourself that you have no reason to worry. God is by your side!

Will Fear Defeat You?

After reading about fear and its crippling effects, are you still going to let fear control your life? Ralph Waldo Emerson said, "Fear defeats more people than any other thing in the world." Is that true about you? Has fear been the greatest cause for defeat in your life? If so, we (Jason and Alex) want to leave you with a few practical steps that will help you say goodbye to fear in your life:

1. Make certain you know Jesus Christ as your Lord and Savior. If you have never repented of your sins and confessed Jesus Christ as Lord and Savior, do that right now. Call out to Christ. Ask Him to forgive you of your sins. John 1:12 states, "But to all who did receive him, who believed in his name, he gave the right to become children of God." And Romans 10:9–10 gives the directive: "If you openly declare that Jesus is Lord and believe in your heart that God raised him from the dead, you will be saved. For it is by believing in your heart that you are made right with God, and it is by openly declaring your faith that you are saved" (NLT).

2. Don't delay. Stop making excuses. Give your fears to God right now. Cry out to Him, "Lord, help me with my fears." Don't think by doing this that God is

going to wave a magic wand, and just like that your fears will vanish. You play a role as well. You must deliberately choose not to live in fear but walk in the faithfulness of Christ.

3. You need to stop being needy, and start depending on God to meet your needs. Your greatest need is to be filled with the Holy Spirit every day (see Ephesians 5:18).

4. Don't make this about fear. Fear is only the by-product of not trusting. Take the opportunity to sit down with a few trusted spiritual advisors (pastor, mentor, or counselor) to discover why you have trust issues in your relationship with God.

5. Make time every day to settle your heart and mind in meditation and prayer to God. It may seem at times like God doesn't hear your prayers. But He does. Come before God boldly in prayer. First John 5:14 states, "And this is the confidence that we have toward him, that if we ask anything according to his will he hears us." Jesus wants to spend time with you now. Take that opportunity. Tell Him what's on your heart.

6. God is Jehovah-Jireh. He is the great provider. God is able. Jesus said, "For your Father knows what you need before you ask him" (Matthew 6:8). Take comfort in knowing and walking in this truth. God will never leave you, nor will He forsake you. He knows what you need before you ask it. Trust in Him.

7. Walk by faith, not by sight. Don't just stay in your comfort zone. Look for opportunities to be challenged. The more you're willing to fail, the stronger you will become. Deuteronomy 31:6 says, "Be strong and courageous. Do not fear or be in dread of them,

for it is the LORD your God who goes with you. He
will not leave you or forsake you."

Friend, as followers of Christ, we are not to live in fear. We are
to be bold and courageous. We are to live victoriously in the risen
Christ! No matter what, make it a habit to say these words spoken
by David each day, "The LORD is on my side; I will not fear. What
can man do to me?" (Psalm 118:6). That's the confidence you
should live out every day of your life!

CHAPTER 3

LIVING BEYOND YOURSELF: THE ROLE OF THE HOLY SPIRIT IN A BELIEVER'S LIFE

You will receive power when
the Holy Spirit comes upon you.
—ACTS 1:8

We live in an age of infomercials. The television and Internet are littered with products to buy—everything from skin-care products, cleaning supplies, weight-loss remedies, and even a Snuggie to keep you warm. There is an endless amount of merchandise out there to help solve whatever problem you may have. And now, with Amazon, you can order something and get it the next day!

But what about faith? Are there any good "products" out there that will bolster the faith of Christians? With all the fear in the world, the constant attacks on religious freedom, and the criticism that Christians face at work and school, what can a Christian do to strengthen his or her faith? Athletes drink Gatorade to refuel and rehydrate. Weight lifters hit the gym. Political candidates need a campaign manager to help them win. But what do Christians need to help them stand strong in their faith?

Christians desperately need the Holy Spirit to stand strong in their faith. But it's important to point out that the Holy Spirit is not a gimmick, a product, or an experiment. The Holy Spirit (the third person of the Godhead) is God.

Billy Graham, in his book *The Holy Spirit: Activating God's Power in Your Life,* prudently said, "If we are to live a life of sanity in our modern world, if we wish to be men and women who can live victoriously, we need this two-sided gift God has offered us: first, the work of the Son of God for us; second, the work of the Spirit of God in us. In this way God has answered mankind's two great cries: the cry for forgiveness and the cry for goodness."[1]

If you want to stand strong in your faith and win the lost to Christ, then the role you allow the Holy Spirit to play in your life will determine everything. To growing in your faith, exercising your spiritual gifts, and to winning the lost—all of this (and more) is dependent on the work of the Holy Spirit in a believer's life. The Holy Spirit is the ultimate and final answer for every Christian. Period!

The Key Player

There are a lot of Christians who are living for the Lord. They attend a good Bible-teaching church and look for ways to serve there. These are important areas for growth in the Christian life, but one thing that needs to be stressed as the utmost importance is the Holy Spirit.

The Christian life isn't about you; rather, it's about God working in and through you. When we put life in perspective, we see how God is moving believers through the power of the Holy Spirit. When we read the book of Acts, we see the acts of the church taking place through individuals like Peter, Paul, and Barnabas. How did they do what they did? How were people saved? How did they perform miracles? Where did they get their boldness? How was the Word of God able to spread so fast? It all came from the Holy Spirit.

What's so sad is how we often overlook the Holy Spirit's work in our lives today. We think of God the Father, the Creator of the heavens and the earth; we think of Jesus Christ, the Redeemer; and then we mention the Holy Spirit and move on. But we must understand that without the Holy Spirit we would never have been given a down payment on our heavenly inheritance.

We should desire that the Spirit of God will so thoroughly possess us that He has total control over us. It is important as Christians not just to say, "I'm a Christian. I'm indwelt by the Holy Spirit," but to recognize the work of the Holy Spirit in our lives. You can know and experience the third person of the Trinity in a way that you never thought possible. Think about how many areas you want to improve in your life. You might want to improve your Spanish, or become more fit, or improve on your recipes. But do you also want to improve on listening and submitting to the Holy Spirit? This, no doubt, takes time. It takes a willingness to seek and desperately pursue the Holy Spirit.

This is what Paul talked about in his letter to the churches in Galatia. He wrote, "But I say, walk by the Spirit, and you will not gratify the desires of the flesh. For the desires of the flesh are against the Spirit, and the desires of the Spirit are against the flesh, for these are opposed to each other, to keep you from doing the things you want to do" (Galatians 5:16–17). Elsewhere Paul says, "Let us also keep *in step* with the Spirit" (Galatians 5:25). When you are sensitive to the conviction of the Holy Spirit and open to Him moving, guiding, and instructing you, then you will live in His sphere of influence. His transformative power will impact every aspect of your life. And the more you walk according to His ways, the less sin will have dominion over you.

> So much of the ineffectiveness and carnality among Christians in the church today is due to them not surrendering to the work of the Holy Spirit.

So much of the ineffectiveness and carnality among Christians in the church today is due to them not surrendering to the work of the Holy Spirit. But when we allow the Holy Spirit to take control, we won't struggle with sin as much, or feel discouraged, or have difficulty studying the Bible or sharing our faith. Any fear consuming us will be overpowered by the Holy Spirit, and all regrets will melt away the moment He comes upon us. That's how amazing the Holy Spirit is! A great way to experience the Holy Spirit is to become more familiar with Him according to the Bible.

The Holy Spirit Is God

Some may ask, "Where in Scripture does it teach us that the Holy Spirit is God?" Great question. For many Christians there is the assumption that the Holy Spirit is kind of an "it," a "force," or some sort of influence. But really the Bible teaches that the Holy Spirit, the third person of the Trinity, is fully God, is personal, can speak, and is knowable. If you're a Christian, the Holy Spirit has been at work in your life. The Spirit of God convicts us of sin, calls us to Jesus, and converts us.[2]

Hebrews 9:14 says that the Holy Spirit is eternal, which means there's never been a time when the Holy Spirit didn't exist. Psalm 104:30 says that the Holy Spirit is co-Creator with the Father and the Son. The Word of God says in Psalm 139:7 that the Spirit of God is omnipresent—He is everywhere. First Corinthians 2:10 says the Spirit of God, the Holy Spirit, knows all the thoughts of God and all the thoughts of humans. We call that omniscience. He knows all things. Think about that. All the thoughts that all the humans in all of history have ever thought and will think—the Holy Spirit knows completely. The Holy Spirit of God knows what every one of us is thinking right now. That's omniscience.

Romans 8:10 tells us that the Holy Spirit gives life. In Ephesians 3:16, Paul tells us that the Holy Spirit also gives strength to the believer, and that He is the Spirit of truth according to Jesus (see John 14). There is a lot more we could say here, but when we're talking about an all-powerful, all-knowing, all-wise, and eternal being, we are describing the characteristics of the Holy Spirit, who is God.

If we look at Ephesians 1:3–14, we will see the role each person of the Trinity played in salvation. God originated salvation before the foundation of the world. After verse 7, Jesus, who is the Redeemer, comes to earth to take away the sins of the world (to bring us back to Him). Following verse 11, we see the work of the Holy Spirit who indwells and seals the believer.

THE HOLY SPIRIT IS:

God—1 Corinthians 3:16

Eternal—Hebrews 9:14

Omniscient—1 Corinthians 2:10–11

Omnipresent—Psalm 139:7

Omnipotent—Genesis 1:2

Holy—Ephesians 4:30

NAMES OF THE HOLY SPIRIT:

Spirit of Grace—Hebrews 10:29

Spirit of Truth—John 14:17; 15:26

Spirit of Life—Romans 8:2

Spirit of Promise—Ephesians 1:13

Spirit of God—1 Corinthians 3:16

Helper, Comforter, or Advocate—John 14:16, 26; 16:7

REPRESENTATIONS OF THE HOLY SPIRIT:

Dove—Matthew 3:16

Wind—John 3:8

Fire—Matthew 3:11

Oil—2 Corinthians 1:21; 1 John 2:27

Water—John 3: 5

Seal—Ephesians 1:13

Streams of living water—John 7:38

Deposit—2 Corinthians 1:22

Thus, each person of the Trinity has a magnificent, powerful, and meaningful role in the salvation that we have in Christ. It has been said that it takes the whole Trinity to make a Christian, just as the complete Godhead participated in the creation of the universe. In salvation, the Father sent the Son, the Son paid the price, and then the Spirit was sent to call and convert the sinner. The Trinity has been operative in the life of every person who is a true believer. Isn't that a beautiful picture?

The Holy Spirit Is a Person

Another point to understand is that the Holy Spirit is a person. He is not some fuzzy, nebulous fog, or an energy source. The Holy Spirit possesses a personality (see Romans 15:30) and has perfect knowledge of all things (see 1 Corinthians 2:10–11). As intimate as your mother's knowledge is of you, the Spirit of God knows everything about you (see Psalm 139).

It's the Spirit of God who imparts to you abilities, strengths, and even interests. This is what is called spiritual gifts that are for the work of ministry. That's why every believer should realize that he or she has received gifts from the Spirit. Over time, we often flesh that out, we sharpen it, and we strengthen it, which is why the apostle Paul opened his letter to the Romans by stating, "For I long to see you, that I may impart to you some *spiritual gift* to strengthen you" (Romans 1:11). When the person of the Holy Spirit imparts a spiritual gift to you (as He does for all believers), that means He has designated you for a specific task. He has given you these gifts because He loves you. He desires to use you. Take some time to familiarize yourself with and enrich yourself on the spiritual gifts found in Romans 12, Ephesians 4, and 1 Corinthians 12.

To help you tap into the Spirit, let's dive into four key biblical aspects (indwelling, convicting, empowering, and guiding) that describe the work of the Holy Spirit in a believer's life. As you learn, we pray that you will receive a powerful anointing from the Holy Spirit!

The Holy Spirit Indwells the Believer

When a person (sinner) repents of his sin and asks Jesus to come into his life, he is (at that moment) indwelt by the Holy Spirit. But what is meant by using the words *dwelt* or *dwelling*? It simply means that the Holy Spirit is inside that person, and he or she is in the Spirit. Romans 8:9 says, "You are, however, not in the flesh but in the Spirit, if in fact the Spirit of God dwells in you. Anyone who does not have the Spirit of Christ does not belong to him." We are also told in 1 Corinthians 3:16, "Do you not know that you are God's temple and that God's Spirit dwells in you?" (ESV).

Ron Rhodes explains the indwelling of the Holy Spirit (in terms of salvation) in this way:

> Paul said God has given us the Holy Spirit as a deposit of what is to come (2 Corinthians 5:5, NIV). The Greek word translated *deposit* refers to a pledge that guaranteed final possession of an item. It was sometimes used of an engagement ring, which acted as a guarantee that the marriage would take place. The Holy Spirit is a deposit in the sense that His presence in our lives guarantees over eventual transformation and glorification into the likeness of Christ's glorified resurrection body (Philippians 3:21). The Holy Spirit in us is a guarantee of what is to come.[3]

There are several Scriptures that shed light on the regenerating power of the Holy Spirit that transforms a sinner, who was once dead but has been made alive in Christ:

> But when the goodness and loving kindness of God our Savior appeared, he saved us, not because of works done

by us in righteousness, but according to his own mercy, by *the washing of regeneration and renewal of the Holy Spirit*, whom he poured out on us richly through Jesus Christ our Savior, so that being justified by his grace we might become heirs according to the hope of eternal life. (Titus 3:4–7)

In him you also, when you heard the word of truth, the gospel of your salvation, and believed in him, were *sealed with the promised Holy Spirit*, who is the guarantee of our inheritance until we acquire possession of it, to the praise of his glory. (Ephesians 1:13–14)

And do not grieve the Holy Spirit of God, by whom you were *sealed* for the day of redemption. (Ephesians 4:30)

Ligonier Ministries has an article on their website that does a wonderful job explaining what Paul meant by the word *sealed*:

When we think of seals, we may picture the seal on a bottle of Tylenol. The elaborate sealing developed for that and similar products came after the deadly results of criminal tampering with the contents. God's sealing also protects against tampering. The Spirit is our shield and guardian. The Lord knows and keeps those who are His (2 Timothy 2:19; John 10:27–28). God's people are sealed with the living God (Revelation 7:2, 4; 9:4). The Spirit as our seal keeps us personally, not mechanically. He keeps us for our inheritance by keeping us believing (1 Peter 1:5–7). We may grieve the Spirit of God by whom we are kept till the day of redemption, and the Spirit may chastise us;

He will certainly prove our faith through fiery trials, but always with the purpose of presenting us at last to God.[4]

Remember, dear Christian: The Holy Spirit indwells you. He purchased you and has given you the assurance that your salvation has been bought and paid for. You belong to God, and He will never let you go!

The Holy Spirit Convicts the Believer

Another important role the Holy Spirit plays in a believer's life is conviction. The Spirit convicts us of our sin. He shows us the errors of our ways. When we disobey Him, we grieve (sadden) the Holy Spirit (see Ephesians 4:30). We are not to prevent Him from working in our lives (see 1 Thessalonians 5:19), but to accept His leadership and bring glory to God.

One of the best books I (Jason) have read about the Holy Spirit was written by Dr. Bill Bright (founder of Campus Crusade for Christ), called *How You Can Be Filled with the Holy Spirit.* In the chapter, "Why Is the Average Christian Not Filled with the Spirit?" Dr. Bright responds by stating:

> The worldly or carnal Christian certainly experiences the conviction of the Holy Spirit and will not continue in his sins indefinitely; otherwise, he is possibly not a Christian at all. However, defeated and fruitless, he depends on self-effort to live the Christian life instead of drawing on the supernatural, inexhaustible resources of the Holy Spirit. Grasping self-interest in one hand and groping for God's blessing with the other, this person fails again and again to live the Christian life in the fullness and power of the Holy Spirit.[5]

We live in a dark and sinful world. And satan will do anything in his power to cause you to ignore the conviction of the Holy Spirit and to give into your fleshly desires. But take comfort. The Holy Spirit indwells you and will give you the power to resist satan and temptation.

The Holy Spirit Empowers the Believer

Prior to ascending to heaven, Jesus gathered His followers and told them, "But you will receive power when the Holy Spirit has come upon you, and you will be my witnesses in Jerusalem and in all Judea and Samaria, and to the end of the earth" (Acts 1:8). The word *power* is the Greek word *dunamis*, which is where we get the word dynamite. Jesus said that for His disciples to become His witnesses, they must first receive the explosive power of the Holy Spirit.

Paul commands every believer to "not be drunk with wine ... but be *filled* with the Holy Spirit" (Ephesians 5:18). We are to pray and ask the Holy Spirit to empower us each day, asking for a new filling of the Holy Spirit's power in our lives. We ask to gain wisdom, love, and strength—and to be the bold witnesses that God has called us to be.

The power of the Holy Spirit makes all the difference in the world. The New Testament mentions over two hundred times that God will give the believer power. In Matthew 28:18, Jesus says, "All authority ... has been given to me." There's authority in the powerful name of Jesus. When Jesus (who has all authority) gives us the Holy Spirit, our attitude shouldn't be a defeatist one. We don't say, "No, I can't," or, "I don't know what to do." No. When we are empowered by the Spirit, we say what Paul said in Philippians 4:13: "I can do all things through him who strengthens me." This ability is supernatural because it comes from the Holy Spirit.

Think about Peter. Here was a man who was afraid and yet bold in many ways. He did a lot of great things, but the difference between Peter before the day of Pentecost (see Acts 2) and after is as different as night and day. What we see throughout the book of Acts is Peter doing unbelievable things. Why? What was the difference? Peter surrendered his life to the Holy Spirit. He wanted nothing more than to be filled with the Spirit's power.

Another great example of a person mightily used by the Holy Spirit is none other than D. L. Moody (1837–1899). He is arguably the greatest evangelist of the nineteenth century. When he was preaching the gospel in England, one of the pastors protested his revivals by questioning, "Why do we need this Mr. Moody? He's uneducated. Who does he think he is anyway? Does he think he has a monopoly on the Holy Spirit?" Upon hearing this rude comment, another pastor stood in Mr. Moody's defense and replied, "No, but the Holy Spirit has a monopoly on D. L. Moody."[6]

Maybe you've been grieving or quenching the work of the Holy Spirit. Maybe you've been crippled because of fear. Whatever it is, before you move on, ask for the filling of the Holy Spirit right now. Don't live another day without His empowerment.

The Holy Spirit Guides the Believer

In John 16:13, Jesus said this about the Holy Spirit: "When the Spirit of truth comes, he will guide you into all the truth." The Holy Spirit is truth. He will not lead you to sin; rather, He will lead you out of it. Think of the Holy Spirit as your teacher or instructor. His job is to teach you the Bible (see 2 Timothy 3:16–17) and instruct you on how to live. Galatians 5:16 says, "But I say, walk by the Spirit, and you will not gratify the desires of the flesh."

The Holy Spirit also distributes the various gifts and abilities in the body of Christ. First Corinthians 12:11 tells us, "All these [spiritual gifts] are empowered by one and the same Spirit, who apportions to each one individually as he wills."

The day will come when Jesus will say, "Behold, I am coming soon, bringing my recompense with me, to repay each one for what he has done" (Revelation 22:12). The day will come, dear Christian, when you will stand before the judgment seat of Christ, and you are going to have to give an account as a steward of the gifts God has given you. And everything that was done in the Holy Spirit will last, but everything that was done in your own strength will be burned up (see 1 Corinthians 3–4). Paul describes the works done in the flesh as wood, hay, and stubble, but the works done in the Spirit are described as precious stones and metal.

Listen, dear friend: It matters. It matters a great deal. It matters not only that you know Jesus as your Savior, but also that you yearn for the filling of the Holy Spirit's power in your life. The choice is up to you: whether to be guided by the Spirit or to rely on your own strength. But if you are going to live beyond yourself, then it is vital that you understand the role of the Holy Spirit in your daily life. He is the one who indwells us, convicts us, empowers us, and guides us.

CHAPTER 4

THE MOST NEGLECTED THING IN AMERICA: THE BIBLE

As a deer pants for flowing streams,
so pants my soul for you, O God.
—KING DAVID (PSALM 42:1)

What if we (Jason and Alex) told you that less than 20 percent of employees working in fast-food restaurants washed their hands after using the restroom? How would you take that? Would you be disgusted? That would gross us out! But what if we were to tell you that less than 20 percent of Christians read the Bible every day? How would you take that? Would it bother you?

Over 60 percent of Americans say that the Bible is the most influential book in history. In 2016, more than twenty-five million Bibles were purchased in America, and yet less than a quarter of Christians read the Bible daily. The fact is that most Americans own several Bibles, but few want the Bible to have ownership over them.[1]

The fact is that most Americans own several Bibles, but few want
the Bible to have ownership over them.

We (Jason and Alex) love to buy Bibles and hand them out as
gifts. But do we treasure the Bible as the ultimate gift written by
God to us? There are so many resources on the Internet, amazing
Bible apps that one can download for free, and a gazillion books
and videos about the Bible at a person's disposal. Yet despite all
this, most Christians (in America) aren't reading the Bible.

There's an 80 percent chance that you're in the category of
Christians who don't read the Bible daily. We commend you for
picking this book up, but we also want to encourage you to make
reading the Bible a daily ritual. There is no way for you to have a
strong faith if you aren't in the Word of God. In this book, thus
far, we've discovered that it's next to impossible to have a strong
faith if your life is consumed with doubt and fear. And there's no
negating the fact that a life not filled with the Holy Spirit's power
is a fruitless life.

What can we expect from a Christian who doesn't try to spend
time in the Bible? Notice how Paul described what the Word of
God does for a believer: "All Scripture is breathed out by God
and *profitable* for teaching, for reproof, for correction, and for
training in righteousness, that the man of God may be *complete*,
equipped for every good work" (2 Timothy 3:16–17).

Did you catch that? When you spend time in God's Word, it
will be profitable to your soul. Like physical exercise is beneficial
for your body, so too is the Word of God beneficial for your soul.
But that's not all. Digging into God's Word also trains you (provides instruction) on how to form proper habits of behavior so

that you are qualified and able to live out your faith in your daily life.

But that's not what's happening. What we are seeing is that the lack of diligent readers of the Bible has resulted in over 80 percent of Christians being biblically illiterate. Woodrow Kroll (former Bible teacher for Back to the Bible), commented, "When we speak of creeping Bible illiteracy in America, we are not talking about the inability to read but the choice not to read. … This failure to read the Bible consistently, or to hear its truth consistently, is the major factor in Bible illiteracy in America. It is an epidemic in … America."[2]

Let's take a closer look at this troubling trend and hopefully come to understand why Christians aren't reading the Bible.

Bible Disengagement

Outreach Magazine publishes a list of the one hundred fastest-growing churches in America every year. About an hour from where I (Alex) live is one of the churches listed. As a matter of fact, this church has been on the list for several years as one of the fastest-growing churches in America. So my wife, Angie, and I went. We wanted to see why the church was growing so fast. We stayed for two services. The church was nice, the greeters were helpful, and the pastor was a good speaker. The only problem was—and it's a big one—there was not one Scripture reference in either service. Not one.

Let's put this in perspective, shall we? How many times have you gone to your favorite restaurant and they forgot to serve the food on their menu? Never. I (Jason) had just taken my family to Chick-fil-A the night before. We walked up to the counter,

STAND STRONG IN YOUR FAITH

ordered from the menu, and paid for our meals. We didn't get burgers or pizza. We got chicken. They served us the food we ordered from their menu. That would be true for any Chick-fil-A franchise we walk into.

When we go to church, what should be on the menu every single time? The Word of God. When you enter any evangelical church (whenever and wherever), you should expect to be served the Word of God. But considering that people are more interested in being entertained and less excited to spend a half hour (or more) in the Bible, many pastors make the mistake of giving them a little of the Bible and a whole lot of nothing.

Telling jokes and unforgettable stories seems to be the key ingredient for sermon prep these days. People have come to expect a sermon series based off a verse in the Bible, with little exegetical (explanatory) teaching from it. This has contributed to the superficial culture in the church that has become disenchanted with the Bible. It seems that more churches look to entertain rather than feed people from the Word of God.

I (Jason) ran across a blog of a pastor who expressed this concern in a colorful way:

> Pastor Dave's church wasn't dissimilar from those that probably dot the suburban landscape in your town; those shiny, sexy, big box store complexes adorned with slick, colorful graphics and state of the art production facilities; pristine buildings with all kinds of wonderfully themed, deftly crafted environments for kids and teens; places with every amenity and every variety of eye candy the Christian consumer could think to ask for. In other words, it's The Church as product, perfected and packaged and franchised out. But get past the dazzling light

shows and the constantly elevated cathartic emotion of the Sunday services; go beneath the flash and din of the sixty minute, big screen rock show euphoria—and you often find there's very little else there. The veneer is gorgeous for sure, but beneath that it's all particle board and duct tape. The American Church is growing prettier but more and more hollow.[3]

Many church leaders are of the belief that entertainment grows churches. The children's ministry needs to look like a theme park. The worship band has to be loud, current, and edgy. The sermon can't be longer than twenty-two minutes flat, with a feel-good message.

While some entertainment-driven churches are seeing growth (like the one Alex visited), the problem is that they are growing for the wrong reasons. If the whole goal is to pack people into the church and entertain them to hell—well, then, that's a poor execution of the Great Commission. What is more, churches that neglect teaching and directing people in the Bible eventually fizzle out. The growth is initial but not sustainable.

What the research shows is that 71 percent of growing churches are led by pastors who read the Bible daily, compared to 19 percent from declining churches. When it came to the congregation, the study revealed that 46 percent of growing churches read the Bible weekly, with only 26 percent of declining churches doing the same.[4]

At the end of the day, a farmer will never harvest crops from his fields if he never planted seeds in the first place. Likewise, churches will not grow (numerically and spiritually) if the Word of God isn't planted in every ministry, outreach, and soul that attends.

The Top-Five Excuses for Not Reading the Bible

Think about the worst excuses you have ever heard. Now think back on some of the lamest excuses you have uttered yourself. The thing about excuses is that there's always an excuse to use them. Take, for instance, a few of the lamest excuses given by friends and family members for not showing up to a wedding:

- "I couldn't get anyone to watch my dog."
- "I thought I was going to be out of town that weekend."
- "My kids get carsick."
- "I lost my wallet and was afraid I might get pulled over."
- "My kids had soccer practice."

Those are some lame excuses, don't you think? But what about the excuses we give for not reading the Bible? Yeah, don't act like you've never made up some lame excuse why you haven't been reading your Bible. We all make excuses.

We (Jason and Alex) are going to give you the top-five excuses why Christians don't read the Bible. As we mentioned above, churches that don't teach consistently from the Bible have become a liability for Christians. However, your pastor is not solely responsible. At the end of the day, if you are not reading the Bible, that's on you. Don't get us wrong—we know that you *want* to read the Bible. We understand that. But what we are getting at is, if you *want* to read the Bible, then *why are you avoiding it?*

Again, there's an 80 percent chance that what we are talking about here relates directly to you. If not, then keep up the great work. But if you are a Christian who has neglected the daily reading of the Bible, we hope you will listen up, and as we lay out the top-five excuses, maybe one (or more) will stand out to you and motivate you to get into the Word!

First Excuse: "I Love My Sin"

There's the old saying, "The Bible will keep you from sin, or sin will keep you from the Bible." Sin is a barrier between you and a holy God. The Bible warns us of our sinful desires, and so if we are not willing to give up our sin, then we're not going to get into the Word of God. The famed evangelist, Billy Sunday, once said, "The reason you don't like the Bible, you old sinner, is because it knows all about you."[5]

When people crave sin, they're not going to be hungry for God's Word. Envy, strife, doubt, sexual sin, gossiping—all forms of sin will inhibit our spiritual desires to want to spend time with God. Isaiah 59:2 declares, "But your iniquities have made a separation between you and your God, and your sins have hidden his face from you so that he does not hear." One way to help you break the sin in your life is to turn to the Word: "Therefore put away all filthiness and rampant wickedness and receive with meekness the *implanted word*, which is able to save your souls" (James 1:21).

Second Excuse: "I Don't Have the Time"

It doesn't matter who you are. We all have twenty-four hours in a day to sleep, work, eat, and do whatever it is we do. If you say you don't have time to spend in the Word, that is only because you don't want to have time with God. We're not trying to be harsh here. We are speaking truth. And the truth is that until you face the reality that you have an intimacy problem with God, you're going to keep making excuses that you just don't have the time. We make time for stuff that is important to us, like binging on Netflix, playing Xbox for hours, or watching NFL games all Sunday long. The truth is that it's not about time; rather, it's about *lacking the desire to want to spend time with God.*

Look at your life right now, and ask yourself, "Why am I making time for _____? What am I willing to rearrange in my schedule to make time with God?" Remember, the more time you spend with Jesus, the more you will emulate Him. David prayed, "As a deer pants for flowing streams, so pants my soul for you, O God" (Psalm 42:1). Elsewhere, the psalmist writes, "But I have calmed and quieted my soul, like a weaned child with its mother; like a weaned child is my soul within me" (Psalm 131:2). May you have that same heart's desire for God as David did!

Third Excuse: "I'm Too Tired"

I (Jason) would get this excuse a lot when I was working with students. One time when I was leading a camp, my leaders and I had set a time for Bible devotions every morning before breakfast. On one of the days, I told the leaders to make it optional for their small groups. They had a choice: get an extra hour of sleep or start the day in the Word of God and prayer. Guess how many students out of a hundred fifty showed up? Twenty. That was it. When breakfast rolled around, I stood outside the cafeteria greeting students. One by one they told me how they wanted to be at Bible devotions but were so tired.

This kind of reminds me of what Jesus told Peter, James, and John when they were in the garden of Gethsemane. Jesus told them to watch and pray, but upon returning three separate times, Jesus found them sleeping (see Matthew 26:36–46). Like Jesus said, "The spirit is willing, but the flesh is weak" (Matthew 26:41).

Do you think Michael Phelps would have won twenty-eight medals if he chose sleep over training? The bottom line is this: Are you going to keep giving into your flesh, or are you going to get disciplined and strengthen your faith? The Bible commands all of us to train ourselves for godliness (see 1 Timothy 4:7). That is not an option. It is a command. What are you waiting for?

Fourth Excuse: "The Bible Is Too Confusing"

If you're reading through the book of Leviticus for the first time or attempting to master the theology of God's sovereignty and divine election in Romans 9–11, then, yeah, we get why you are confused. But to say the Bible is confusing isn't a fair statement. Of course, there are difficult passages in the Bible, but that doesn't mean you give up trying to understand the whole of it. It takes hard work and rigorous study.

Perhaps it has nothing to do with the Bible not making sense. Maybe it's the opposite. Maybe it's what does make sense that has caused you to pull away from the Bible. Søren Kierkegaard, the nineteenth-century Danish theologian, said it brilliantly: "The Bible is very easy to understand. But we Christians are a bunch of scheming swindlers. We pretend to be unable to understand it because we know very well that the minute we understand, we are obliged to act accordingly."[6]

Maybe it's more of a heart issue than an intellectual one. James warns of this kind of behavior with Scripture. He gives the illustration of a mirror: "For if anyone is a hearer of the word and not a doer, he is like a man who looks intently at his natural face in a mirror. For he looks at himself and goes away and at once forgets what he was like" (James 1:23–24). And Psalm 119:18 says, "Open my eyes, that I may behold wondrous things out of your law." If you ask the Spirit of God to open your heart and help you understand the Word, then He will help you do just that.

Fifth Excuse: "It's Boring"

For some Christians, reading the Bible is like watching paint dry. No matter how hard they try, they just can't get into it. We hear from guys all the time who say they don't read. It's boring to them. But they have no problem being entertained by watching a game, playing on their phone, or vegging out watching the news. Here is the deal with boredom: If you are having a hard time reading the Bible, it's because you lack a love for it. It's that simple. Somewhere along the way, you lost interest. And the more impartial you are to the Bible, the colder your heart will be toward it.

The Bible is no longer seen as a love letter; rather, it is viewed as just a big book of ancient stories. Yeah, you believe the Bible is the infallible Word of God, but the excitement and thrill of it has been lost. A great passage that expresses a deep appreciation for the powerfulness of God's Word is found in Psalm 19:7–14:

> The law of the LORD is perfect,
> > reviving the soul;
> the testimony of the LORD is sure,
> > making wise the simple;
> the precepts of the LORD are right,
> > rejoicing the heart;
> the commandment of the LORD is pure,
> > enlightening the eyes;
> the fear of the LORD is clean,
> > enduring forever;

the rules of the LORD are true,
and righteous altogether.
More to be desired are they than gold,
even much fine gold;
sweeter also than honey
and drippings of the honeycomb.
Moreover, by them is your servant warned;
in keeping them there is great reward.
Who can discern his errors?
Declare me innocent from hidden faults.
Keep back your servant also from presumptuous sins;
let them not have dominion over me!
Then I shall be blameless,
and innocent of great transgression.
Let the words of my mouth and the meditation of my heart
be acceptable in your sight,
O LORD, my rock and my redeemer.

Can you hear the love David has for the Word of God here? He articulates that God's Word is not only better than the finest gold, but it is also sweeter than the sweetest thing on earth!

This kind of love for God's Word doesn't just happen. It comes through trials and various tribulations. It comes by trusting God and leaning on His Word for guidance and strength. No doubt, this was all too familiar to David. And in the end, David found that the passions of this world paled in comparison to the passion for God's Word.

> "... one chief reason that I have been kept in happy useful service is that I have been a lover of Holy Scripture."
> —*George Mueller*

George Mueller, a man who lived by great faith establishing orphanages throughout England in the nineteenth century, said this about the Bible: "I believe that the one chief reason that I have been kept in happy useful service is that I have been a lover of Holy Scripture. It has been my habit to read the Bible through four times a year; in a prayerful spirit, to apply it to my heart, and practice what I find there. I have been for sixty-nine years a happy man."[7]

Don't you want this kind of love that King David and George Mueller had for the Word of God? If so, then there are a few practical tips to get you back on track (more on this in chapter 7).

First, pray for a desire to want to learn and understand the Bible. Jesus says, "When anyone hears the word of the kingdom and does not understand it, the evil one comes and snatches away what has been sown in his heart" (Matthew 13:19). It is important to focus your heart and passion toward the Bible and let nothing come in between that love. Dr. George H. Guthrie writes, "Once our hearts are receptive to the Word, we can hear the motivations offered us in Scripture. Among other motives, we read the Bible."[8] Here are some motives:

- to experience consistent joy (see Psalm 119:111).
- to sort out our thoughts and motivations (see Hebrews 4:12).
- to guard ourselves from sin and error (see Ephesians 6:11–17; 1 Peter 2:1–2).
- to know God in a personal relationship (see 1 Corinthians 1:21; Galatians 4:8–9; 1 Timothy 4:16).
- to know truth and to think clearly about what God says is valuable (see 2 Peter 1:21).

- to be built up as a community with other believers (see Acts 20:32; Ephesians 4:14–16).
- to reject conformity to the world as we renew our minds (see Romans 12:1–2; 1 Peter 2:1–2).
- to experience God's freedom, grace, peace, and hope (see John 8:32; Romans 15:4; 2 Peter 1:2).
- to live well for God, expressing our love for Him (see John 14:23–24; Romans 12:1–2; 1 Thessalonians 4:1–8).
- to minister to Christ-followers and to those who have yet to respond to the gospel, experiencing God's approval for work well done (see Joshua 1:8; 2 Timothy 2:15; 3:16–17).[9]

Second, believe and treasure the Bible as the very Word of God. Peter writes, "Knowing this first of all, that no prophecy of Scripture comes from someone's own interpretation. For no prophecy was ever produced by the will of man, but men spoke from God as they were carried along by the Holy Spirit" (2 Peter 1:20–21). God spoke through His people so that we could have written revelation about Him and His plan of redemption. Take comfort in knowing that you can trust the Word of God.

Third, allow the Word of God to be implanted in your life. James writes, "Therefore put away all filthiness and rampant wickedness and receive with meekness the implanted word, which is able to save your souls" (James 1:21). Allow the Word of God to teach you, convict you, and shape you as you become more like Jesus Christ (see Ephesians 4:13).

Fourth, pursue a passion to be trained in the Word of God. Paul writes, "All Scripture is breathed out by God and profitable for teaching, for reproof, for correction, and for training in righteousness, that the man of God may be complete, equipped for every good work" (2 Timothy 3:16–17). It's absolutely amazing what the Word of God can do in your life. It makes you wiser, it makes you holier, and it makes you a thorough worker for God. There is nothing quite like it!

Fifth, look to be nourished, sanctified, renewed, satisfied, strengthened, built up, and filled with wisdom in the Word of God. When you love God's Word, you will eat from it every day and be blessed and filled! You will:

- be nourished (see 1 Peter 1:23; 2:2),
- be sanctified (see John 17:16–17),
- be renewed (see Ephesians 4:24),
- be satisfied (see Colossians 3:16),
- be strengthened (see Ephesians 6:13–18),
- be built up (see Acts 20:32), and
- be filled with wisdom (see Psalm 19:7–11; 119).

Martin Luther wrote this in his excellent book *On Christian Liberty*: "The soul can do without everything except the word of God, without which none at all of its wants are provided for." May you not be just another Christian who occasionally reads the Bible; may you be a Christian who falls in love with it more each day!

> If you are to stand strong in your faith and be a confident and passionate believer, then you must make reading God's Word a priority in your life.

As you get serious about getting back into the Bible, make sure you find an accountability partner who will hold your feet to the fire. This will prevent you from deterring and falling back into your old habits. If you are to stand strong in your faith and be a confident and passionate believer, then you must make reading God's Word a priority in your life. We must learn to treasure it, to love it, to read it, and to apply it. In the next chapter, we will deal with Christians' doubts about the Bible and lay out a strong case why you can trust it.

CHAPTER 5

HOW CAN I KNOW THE BIBLE IS TRUE?

Heaven and earth will pass away,
but my words will endure forever.

—MARK 13:31

S ing with us, "The B-I-B-L-E, yes, that's the book for me. I stand alone on the Word of God, the B-I-B-L-E." Don't you just love that little Christian tune that most of us learned back in the Sunday school days? Or how about the acronym for BIBLE: Basic Instruction Before Leaving Earth. Clever, huh?

Even though these are fun, do you believe the Bible is the Word of God? How do you know you can trust what it says?

Without question, the Bible is the ultimate resource for any human being. It is vital to the growth of any Christian. However, the massive neglect of reading the Bible among Christians has left a generation of "Christians" who can't tell you one way or another why they can trust in the Bible. In the last chapter, we gave you the top-five excuses why Christians rarely read the Bible, and in this chapter, we address an underlying issue that feeds into any one of those excuses—it has to do with doubt. Whether or not you are aware of it, Christians doubting the veracity of Scripture has become a big-time issue in the church today.

We (Jason and Alex) have spent a great deal of our lives defending the Bible and equipping Christians in apologetics (defending the faith [see 1 Peter 3:15]). If people could wrap their minds around the fact that God gave them His inspired Word, and if they desired to live it and learn it, it would not just radically change their lives, but would also change their families, their work environments, their neighborhoods, their friends, their cities, and their culture.

In the book of Acts, there are many passages that describe the powerful spread of the Word of God. But in Acts 6:7, we read how the Word of God not only increased and multiplied the number of disciples of Christ, but even converted Jewish priests too: "And the word of God continued to increase, and the number of the disciples multiplied greatly in Jerusalem, and a great many of the priests became obedient to the faith."

> Hands down, the Bible is the most influential book in history.
> Nothing comes close to its transformative power.

Hands down, the Bible is the most influential book in history. Nothing comes close to its transformative power. Many of its authors have been murdered. Scrolls have been burned. Emperors and kings have fought wars in attempts to destroy it and silence the Christians. And yet the Bible is still here changing lives, kingdoms, and nations. Jesus said, "Heaven and earth will pass away, but my words will not pass away" (Mark 13:31).

That's why gaining confidence in the Bible and becoming a confident defender of its trustworthiness is crucial. Hence, the purpose of this chapter. We want to embolden you to know with assurance and give you a simple way to share with others why they too can trust in the Bible. But before we dive in, we would like to take the opportunity to share a little bit about our journey with the Bible.

I (Jason), as far back as I can remember, have always been emotionally drawn to the Bible. I'm not what you would call a fideist (someone who accepts things solely based on faith or revelation). I have always been inquisitive, skeptical, and investigative in my approach to spiritual matters. My upbringing was mixed with Catholicism (on the Jimenez side), with a splash of Four-square denominational practices and a twist of Calvary Chapel (nondenominational). As you can tell, my childhood was very—shall we say—eclectic.

Though my parents believed in the Bible, and I would see them (on occasion) reading it, it wasn't at the forefront of our home. I would ask my family questions about the Bible, Jesus, salvation, and about what makes other religions different, but I never seemed to get answers that were backed up with facts. To me, it always seemed like my family believed the Bible simply because it was the right thing to do.

That wasn't enough for me. Quite frankly, it was unacceptable. I didn't want to believe in something just because my family did. So if I wasn't going to get answers to my questions from them, then I needed to look elsewhere. Of course, predating the Internet, it was a lot more work finding the right books in libraries and magazines.

As I studied, I started to discover answers to my questions. I began to see how overwhelming the preponderance of evidence is for the Bible. And I must say, it brought me to tears. The amount of evidence we have for the Bible is staggering! Coming to this place in my life, as a teenager, radically changed my life. When I lost my mom in a car accident at the age of fifteen, I was at a place where I could trust and look to the Word of God for comfort.

I (Alex) was a college student when I became a Christian. I believed in evolution and thought it was groovy to call myself a philosophical anarchist (a person who rejects government power). I didn't believe in rules and sought to convert my friends. My heroes were John Lennon, Jim Morrison, and Friedrich Nietzsche. But the strangest thing happened to me one day—I began reading the Bible. No one told me to read it; I just did. And the more I read, the more I realized how sinful and wrong I was and that I needed Jesus Christ. That's the power of God's Word. It changed my life, and we know it can change yours too!

Without further delay, here is an acronym that I (Jason) came up with a few years ago. I wanted to provide my audiences with a simple way to remember and share why they can trust the Bible. It is the acronym BIBLE, which stands for Brand, Inspiration, Background, Literature, and Errorless Teaching.

Brand
Inspiration
Background
Literature
Errorless Teaching

Brand: The Continuity of the Bible

The first thing we want to look at is the brand. Everything has a brand. McDonald's has a brand, Apple has a brand, Microsoft has a brand, and Nike has its own distinct brand. And guess what? The Bible has a brand too.

When we suggest the Bible has a brand, we are not reducing it to a product or cheapening its contents. What we are saying is that the Bible has a unique trademark. Its brand has a divine origin, which makes the Bible's composition so extraordinary. Dr. William F. Albright, an American archaeologist and Bible scholar, said, "The Bible towers in content above all earlier religious literature and it towers just as impressively over all subsequent literature in a direct simplicity of its message, in the Catholicity of its appeal to all men of all lands and times."[1] Dr. Albright knew what he was talking about because he was a legend when it came to the archaeological discoveries mentioned in the Old and New Testaments. He's known as the Dean of Biblical Archeology.

What's so incredible about the sixty-six books that make up the Bible is their diversity of forty authors. These different authors wrote during different time frames (spanning some fifteen hundred years), in three different languages, and on three different continents. You've got Moses, who was a political leader; David, who was a king; Amos, who was a farmer; and Luke, who was a physician. Paul was a brilliant philosopher and theologian, Peter was a fisherman, and Matthew was a tax collector. With all these different authors, you'd expect discrepancies, disagreements, and contradictions. Yet that is not what we find.

What's so incredible about the sixty-six books that make up the Bible is their diversity of forty authors. These different authors wrote during different time frames (spanning some fifteen hundred years), in three different languages, and on three different continents. You've got Moses, who was a political leader; David, who was a king; Amos, who was a farmer; and Luke, who was a physician. Paul was a brilliant philosopher and theologian, Peter was a fisherman, and Matthew was a tax collector. With all these different authors, you'd expect discrepancies, disagreements, and contradictions. Yet that is not what we find.

> What's so incredible about the sixty-six books that make up the Bible is their diversity of forty authors. With all these different authors, you'd expect discrepancies, disagreements, and contradictions. Yet that is not what we find.

The Bible has a clear, consistent message woven through from Genesis to Revelation: Jesus Christ is the Redeemer. The prophets foretold of the coming Messiah, and the apostles identified and proclaimed the Messiah's message, as well as prophetically pronounced His second coming. That is continuity!

Inspiration: The Authority of the Bible

Now we get into the inspiration of the Bible, which deals with the authority of the Bible. Paul writes in 2 Timothy 3:16, "All Scripture is inspired by God and profitable for teaching, for reproof, for correction, for training in righteousness." The word *inspiration* simply means "God breathed." God spoke (or revealed) His perfect Word to humankind through the instrumentation of the Holy Spirit.

Second Peter 1:21 reads, "For no prophecy was ever produced by the will of man, but men spoke from God as they were carried along by the Holy Spirit." The word *carried* in the Greek conveys the idea of wind through the sails of a boat—to move it forward. Thus, man was the free agent who recorded the revealed Word of God through the Holy Spirit. The writers weren't in a trance or coerced to write the Bible.

God's Inspiration	Revealed the Word
The Holy Spirit's Instrumentation	Carried the Word
Man's Dictation	Recorded the Word

In their excellent book *When Skeptics Ask,* Dr. Noman Geisler and Ronald Brooks offer a great explanation when it comes to the divine and human origin of the Bible. They write:

> The net result is that we have the Word of God written by men of God, inspired not only in its concepts, but in the very words used to express those concepts. The human writers are not mere secretaries, but active agents who express their own experiences, thoughts, and feelings in what they have written. It is not simply a record of revelation, but a revelation itself. It is God's message in written form (Heb. 1:1; 2 Peter 1:21).[2]

Benjamin B. Warfield made sense of inspiration this way: "The Bible is the Word of God in such a sense that its words, though written by men and bearing indelibly impressed upon them the marks of their human origin, were written, nevertheless, under such an influence of the Holy Ghost as to be also the words of God, the adequate expression of His mind and will."[3] Thus, when the Holy Spirit moved upon (inspired) the different authors (human agents), they freely wrote down the inerrant and infallible Word of God.

Background: The Canonicity of the Bible

Next is the background. The Bible was pieced together, copied, and transmitted through the centuries. Much of the debate about the Bible centers around this topic, known as canonicity.

The word *canon* simply means "measuring stick or ruler." As such, the canonicity of the Bible acted as the standard, rule, or measure to ensure that what was placed in it was, in fact, the doctrinal truths of God. Dr. Geisler makes the point, "It is the inspiration of a book which determines its canonicity. God gives the divine authority to a book and men of God receive it. God reveals and His people recognize what He reveals. Canonicity is determined by God and discovered by man."[4]

However, given the fact that there were so many false books and false writings that were in circulation, how was the early church able to identify what was an inspired book and what was not? There were, essentially, five foundational questions or criteria that were implemented to guide the process of discovering what books were inspired by God:

- Criteria #1: Was the book written by a prophet of God?
- Criteria #2: Did the writer confirm his writings with miracles?
- Criteria #3: Does the writer and his message speak the truth of God?
- Criteria #4: Does the book demonstrate the power of God changing lives?
- Criteria #5: Was the book accepted by the early church?

The Hebrew Bible (*Tanakh*) was completed by 400 BC, and less than two hundred years later, we have the Hebrew Scriptures translated into Greek, known as the Septuagint (250–200 BC). By the time of the first century, the Hebrew language was in decline, forcing the Jews to interpret the Hebrew Scriptures into Aramaic (*Targums*). By the time of Jesus' public ministry, He, His apostles, and the New Testament writers all accepted and affirmed the Old

Testament books. Many of them cited most of the Jewish Scriptures as the Word of God. Jesus also cited each section and most of the Old Testament as part of the canon (see Matthew 23:35; 1 Thessalonians 5:27).

By the time Josephus (AD 37–100), a Jewish historian, came on the scene, he mentioned many of the Jewish books, along with details recorded in the writings of the Gospels, and some of the apostles in *The Jewish Wars* and *The Jewish Antiquities.* By AD 90–118 at the Council of Jamnia, the Jewish scholars recognized the thirty-nine books of the Old Testament to be canonical (originated by Rabbi Johanan ben Zakkai). Many of the church fathers, such as Clement, Polycarp, Ignatius, Irenaeus, and Justin Martyr, recognized the divine authority of both the Old and New Testaments as inspired books of God and used them as Scripture in the church.

In the third century, Origen (AD 185–254), studied the collective books of the New Testament and underscored their inspiration of God. By the fourth century, the bishop of Caesarea and great church historian, Eusebius (AD 270–340) articulated the canon of most of the twenty-seven books in his *Church History.* However, it was Athanasius (bishop of Alexandria) who wrote in *Festal Letter* (AD 367) that twenty-seven canonical books make up the New Testament today.

By the time of the Synod of Hippo (AD 393) and Council of Carthage (AD 397), the council decreed the twenty-seven books as divine Scripture. Up to this point in church history, most of the Western and Eastern churches affirmed the New Testament as the canon of Scripture. It wasn't the church who made the New Testament books authoritative, however; they simply affirmed that they were already divinely inspired. Again, the apostles and early church leaders did not choose the canon, but they recognized the canon that the Holy Spirit had indicated and which Christians had been reading and preaching for three centuries.

We can have full confidence that the sixty-six books of the Bible (thirty-nine in the Old Testament and twenty-seven in the New Testament) are inspired by God and convey the true message that we are sinners who are in need of Jesus. Throughout the pages of the Bible, the measuring stick of right and wrong is consistently demonstrated based on the standards given by God. The Bible tells us about life and death, truth and error, and obedience and disobedience. The canon of Scripture is a reference to the fact that there is not one book missing or added that should not be there. The canon of Scripture is exactly what God determined for the church to discover.

Literature: The Authenticity of the Bible

Now we get into the authenticity of the Bible's literature. A look back at historical markings will help us see how well preserved the Bible was kept throughout the centuries.

The Preservation of the Old Testament

After the Septuagint in 250–200 BC, came the Talmudic period (AD 100–500)—a time of teaching and instruction from the *Mishnah* (oral traditions) and *Gemara* (commentaries on the *Mishnah*). Hundreds of well-preserved synagogue scrolls and private copies of the Jewish Scriptures have been discovered during this period.

After the Talmudic period came the Masoretic period (AD 500–950). The Masoretes were Jewish rabbis and scholars who guarded and preserved the Jewish Scriptures. They carry the richest scribal ritualism of meticulously transmitting copies of the Old Testament books. Many of these ancient manuscripts have a word-to-word count that corresponds to specific manuscripts that dated to much earlier times.

> Oldest form of the Bible is Numbers (written on silver leaves), which was discovered in 1979 in Jerusalem and is 2,600 years old.
>
> Oldest fragment of Hebrew Bible (until Dead Sea Scrolls) is "Nash Papyrus," which contains the Ten Commandments and Shema. It is dated first or second century BC (discovered in Egypt in 1902).

Thus, by the time we get to the Dead Sea Scrolls (discovered in 1947), this extraordinary find of the Essene community (Jewish sect from 300 BC–AD 50) pushed back the date of the earliest biblical manuscripts by a thousand years! Up to this point, the Leningrad Codex (AD 1008) was the oldest complete Hebrew Bible.

For the next several years, archaeologists unearthed 28 complete scrolls, 100,000 fragments, 875 manuscripts, and multiple portions of every Hebrew book (except for Esther) in Qumran caves near the Dead Sea. Some of these ancient collections of biblical texts go as far back as to the second temple (AD 70). That's why one of America's foremost archaeologists, William F. Albright (1891–1971), referred to the discovery of the Dead Sea Scrolls as "the greatest archaeological find of modern times." And to think that the Dead Sea Scrolls were accidentally discovered by a Bedouin shepherd boy.

The Preservation of the New Testament

Let's now take a closer look at how authentic the New Testament manuscripts are. First, when examining the manuscripts of the Bible, they are early, more-abundant, and more-accurately copied manuscripts than any book from the ancient world. There are some 5,800 manuscripts of the New Testament in Greek (and counting!). The Greek manuscripts are earlier and more accurate than other books from the ancient world with over 99 percent accuracy. In fact, 100 percent of all the basic teaching of the Bible is conveyed in the copies. Not to mention the accuracy of the biblical writers. Dr. Norman Geisler and William Nix put the accuracy of the manuscript copies into perspective:

> When a comparison of the variant readings of the New Testament is made with those of other books that have survived from antiquity, the results are little short of astounding. For instance, although there are 200,000 (and some assert there are 400,000) "errors" among the New Testament manuscripts, these appear in only about 10,000 places, and only about one-sixtieth rise above the level of trivialities. Westcott and Hort, Ezra Abbot, Philip Schaff, and A. T. Robertson have carefully evaluated the evidence and concluded that the New Testament text is 99+ percent pure. A. T. Robertson said, "The real concern is with a thousandth part of the entire text" (which equals 99.9 percent accuracy). Philip Schaff added that only fifty variants were of real significance, and there is no "article of faith or a precept of duty which is not abundantly sustained by other and undoubted passages, or by the whole tenor of Scripture teaching."[5]

From the time of writing, which was within a generation of eyewitnesses, to the age of the copies we have, to the number of copies and how complete these copies are, we are certain that what we have today in our Bible is what was originally written.

This criterion is what historians look at when they determine the authenticity of a text. And three of the most well-attested secular ancient manuscripts accepted by all scholars are *The Annals of Caesar*, along with *The Iliad* and *The Odyssey* by Homer. And yet the most well-attested of Homer's works (*The Iliad*) has 643 copies (which is extremely impressive). And yet the New Testament has some thirty thousand manuscripts in different languages and from different periods of history. No other ancient document comes even close to the manuscripts of the Bible (with less gaps). There is nothing like it in antiquity.

The Muratorian Fragment	Discovered in 1740 and is the oldest-known list of New Testament books.
The Chester Beatty Papyri (AD 120–150)	Supposedly discovered in urns in an Egyptian Coptic Christian cemetery. In 1930–1931, Chester Beatty (American collector) purchased many fragments from a dealer in Egypt. Most of the papyri date to the third century and contain portions of the Gospels, Pauline letters, and most of the book of Revelation.
Codex Vaticanus (mid-fourth century)	Discovered in the 1800s and comes from the Vatican library. It contains nearly all the books of the Bible and is considered to be the oldest nearly complete set in existence.
Codex Sinaiticus (mid-fourth century)	Discovered in 1844 (first journey) and 1859 (third journey). The oldest complete manuscript of the New Testament.
Codex Alexandrinus (fifth century)	May have been a part of the ancient library in Alexandria and contains 773 parchments of the Old and New Testaments, as well as one of the earliest books to use decorative markings.

Errorless Teaching: The Reliability of the Bible

Finally, is the errorless teaching of the Bible. What we mean by *errorless* is that the Bible was originally written with no errors, mistakes, or flaws in it. This is known as the doctrine of inerrancy. If God is perfect and cannot err, then anything He does is perfect; since the Bible is the Word of God, it is therefore without err.

Proverbs 30:5–6 says, "Every word of God proves true; he is a shield to those who take refuge in him. Do not add to his words, lest he rebuke you and you be found a liar." Inerrancy covers both the factual (historical and scientific data), as well as the spiritual affirmations and the intentions of the Bible, which is the divine and final authority of God. The Bible is prophetically, historically, and scientifically accurate.

Prophetical Accuracy

One of the strongest proofs that the Bible is the Word of God is its predictive prophecies. J. Barton Payne lists 1,817 predictions in the Bible: 1,239 in the Old Testament and 578 in the New Testament. Out of the almost 2,000 prophecies, 191 of the prophecies are contributed to the coming Messiah. Here are three main prophecies of Jesus Christ:

1. His birth (see Isaiah 7:14; Micah 5:2; Matthew 1; Luke 2).
2. His death (see Psalm 22; Isaiah 53; Matthew 26–27).
3. His resurrection (see Psalm 2; 16; 110:1; Matthew 28).

According to mathematician P. W. Stoner in his book *Science Speaks*, the probability of sixteen predictions being fulfilled in one man (e.g., Jesus) is 1 in 10^{45}. The probability of Jesus fulfilling forty-eight prophecies is 1 in 10^{157}. What's the point? The point is that Jesus has to be God in order to fulfill prophecy.

Historical Accuracy

Archeological discoveries are great pieces of evidence that support and verify the historical and cultural accuracy of the Old and New Testaments. Just imagine if certain archeological discoveries contradicted the claims of the Bible? What then? If that were true, then the Bible wouldn't be the inspired Word of God because its historical claims are factually untrue. For the sake of time, allow us to give one piece of archeological evidence for both the Old and New Testaments.

Until the summer of 1993, there were no real pieces of evidence to support that King David existed in history. However, Dr. Avraham Biran and his crew were excavating a site located in northern Galilee at the foot of Mt. Hermon and uncovered the remains of a stone slab containing Aramaic inscriptions that read "King of Israel" and "House of David." In recent years, archeologists were finally able to end the dispute over whether the Pool of Bethesda with five porticoes really existed according to John 5:1–15. Furthermore, another disputed site called the Pool of Siloam in John 9:7 was also discovered in 1897.

Scientific Accuracy

It is important to note that though the Bible is not to be read like a science textbook, it doesn't make any scientific mistakes. And that is good, because every science textbook contains errors and is constantly finding new data.

The Bible has taught that the universe had a beginning from the start (see Genesis 1:1; Job 38:4–7; Psalm 33:6; Isaiah 42:5).

In 1543, Copernicus discovered that the earth suspends in empty space, all the while thousands of years ago Job wrote, "He stretches out the north over the void and hangs the earth on nothing" (26:7). Though most of the world thought the earth was flat prior to Copernicus' discovery in 1543, the book of Isaiah (740–680 BC) said, "It is he who sits above the circle of the earth, and its inhabitants are like grasshoppers; who stretches out the heavens like a curtain, and spreads them like a tent to dwell in (40:22)."[6]

We can trust the Scriptures because they came from God. And think of this: Jesus Christ, who rose from the dead, affirmed both the Old and New Testaments. Until the skeptic can eclipse the résumé of Jesus—His virgin-born, sinless life, and the fact that He rose from the dead—we are going to go with Christ's take on Scripture.[7]

How do we know the Bible is true? There is overwhelming evidence to suggest that it is reliable. All we need to do is look at its brand, its inspiration, its background, the literature it contains, and its errorless teaching. If we want to stand strong in our faith and become a believer who is passionate and confident, then we need to be convinced of its sufficiency in our lives. The Bible is vital to the growth of any Christian.

CHAPTER 6

THE CRUX OF HISTORY: DID JESUS RISE FROM THE DEAD?

*If Christ has not been raised, our preaching
is useless and so is your faith.*
—Paul the Apostle (1 Corinthians 15:14)

Why do you believe in Christianity? Why give your life to Jesus Christ? There are dozens of belief systems in the world today competing for the hearts and minds of the people. So why Christianity? What makes it so special?

In this chapter, we are going to talk about the central truth of the Christian faith—the resurrection of Jesus Christ. Jesus Christ didn't stay dead in the tomb but rose from the grave. His resurrection is the citadel of Christianity. There are many things that make Christianity unique in the pantheon of world religions, but the fact that Jesus died and rose from the dead sets it apart from all other religions. Michael Green aptly states:

Christianity does not hold the resurrection to be one among many tenets of belief. Without faith in the resurrection *there would be no Christianity at all*. The Christian church would never have begun; the Jesus-movement would have fizzled out like a damp squib with His execution. Christianity stands or falls with the truth of the resurrection. Once disprove it, and you have disposed of Christianity.[1]

> There are many things that make Christianity unique in the pantheon of world religions, but the fact that Jesus died and rose from the dead sets it apart from all other religions.

The great convert, Paul the apostle, laid out a brilliant account of the resurrection of Jesus Christ in 1 Corinthians 15. Paul openly acknowledged, "If there is no resurrection of the dead, then not even Christ has been raised. And if Christ has not been raised, our preaching is useless and so is your faith. … And if Christ has not been raised, your faith is futile; you are still in your sins. Then those also who have fallen asleep in Christ are lost. If only for this life we have hope in Christ, we are of all people most to be pitied" (1 Corinthians 15:13–14, 17–19 NIV). Paul is hanging everything on Jesus rising from the grave. If Jesus didn't rise, then we are false witnesses. Not only that, but those we thought have gone to heaven after they died, never did. Paul said if Christ is not raised, then we of all people are most miserable.

That's a serious accusation. But, of course, Paul is right. Not all faith claims can be tested and therefore empirically verified or denied. Yet, according to Paul, all a person must do is disprove that the resurrection of Jesus occurred in history and Christianity falls like a house of cards. Dr. William Lane Craig writes:

> Without the belief in the resurrection the Christian faith could not have come into being. The disciples would have remained crushed and defeated men. Even had they continued to remember Jesus as their beloved teacher, his crucifixion would have forever silenced any hopes of his being the Messiah. The cross would have remained the sad and shameful end of his career. The origin of Christianity therefore hinges on the belief of the early disciples that God had raised Jesus from the dead.[2]

That's how quintessential the resurrection is. Yet the liberal theologian Marcus Borg said this about the resurrection: "As a child, I took it for granted that Easter meant that Jesus literally rose from the dead. I now see Easter very differently. For me, it is irrelevant whether or not the tomb was empty. Whether Easter involved something remarkable happening to the physical body of Jesus is irrelevant."[3]

Can you believe what Mr. Borg just said? He's saying that a physical resurrected body is irrelevant to the Christian faith. Not only that, but if Jesus rose from the dead, it still doesn't matter. What? We have news for Mr. Borg: It does matter! Why? Because like David Hume said, dead people don't rise from the dead. But if Jesus did rise from the dead, that means He is God. And if He is God, then Mr. Borg, David Hume, and all the rest of humanity must answer to Him.

There have been a lot of people over the last two thousand

years who have tried to get around the fact that Jesus rose from the dead. People have come and gone throughout history, trying to dismiss and explain away the empty tomb. The reason being because people understand that the resurrection validates the Man and His message. If Jesus rose, He is who He claimed to be—the very Son of God.

We (Jason and Alex) will address these objections or alternate explanations to the historical facts of the resurrection, and provide you, the believer, with the total confidence and assurance that your faith in a resurrected Christ is on solid ground. But before we do that, let's lay out a few of the most popular alternate theories to the resurrection. They are the swoon theory, the stolen body theory, and the hallucination theory.

Objection #1: Swoon Theory

Jesus Faked His Own Death

The swoon theory essentially argues that Jesus faked His own death—He never died on the cross. The theory tries to demonstrate that either Jesus intentionally played dead on the cross or that He may have passed out while hanging there. When Jesus was placed in the cold tomb, it somehow revived Him back to consciousness, where He then shook off His grave clothes, got up, and moved away the stone. Jesus then managed to get past the armed guards and went across town without being recognized, all the while bleeding from His flogging and being nailed to the cross. Nonetheless, Jesus fought through His injuries and was able to regather His disciples and prove that He rose from the grave just like He predicted. The disciples rallied others and launched a religion known today as Christianity.

Response

The more we think about the swoon theory and all that would have to be involved for it to be true, the more ludicrous it sounds. There are two primary problems with this theory. Michael O'Connell tells us, for one thing, that nobody survived crucifixion from about 1000 BC up through the first century when Rome did thousands of executions by crucifixion. This is corroborated by the Jewish historian Josephus. Reportedly, only one man has ever been taken down alive from the cross, but he later died within twenty-four hours.

The second problem with the swoon theory is that it makes Jesus out to be a liar. Here we have the most moral Man in history, who essentially predicated everybody's loyalty on a lie. It just doesn't fit the person of Jesus. There is no respect or allegiance to a person who builds his entire movement on a false resurrection.

The bottom line is that no one survived crucifixion. Even if Jesus were to endure through the pain and the suffering, as we know from the accounts—when they came to break His legs to speed up the death process—He was already dead. Furthermore, we are talking about Jesus Christ here. This is the guy who had been stirring up a lot of commotion for nearly four years, not just with the Romans but with the Jews too. Therefore, Pontius Pilate would have made sure (and he did) that Jesus was, in fact, dead before taking Him down from the cross. Also, Jesus' death was verified with a spear to His side into the pericardial cavity, which released the fluid that had built up around his heart as He hung on the cross. The result was that blood and water flowed out, which indicated that He was already dead. Medically speaking, there is no way Jesus could have survived the crucifixion.

Objection #2: Stolen Body Theory

The Disciples Stole Jesus' Body

In the stolen body theory, it is believed that the disciples stole the body of Jesus after He was placed in the tomb. Matthew 28:11–15 reads:

> While they were going, behold, some of the guard went into the city and told the chief priests all that had taken place. And when they had assembled with the elders and taken counsel, they gave a sufficient sum of money to the soldiers and said, "Tell people, 'His disciples came by night and stole him away while we were asleep.' And if this comes to the governor's ears, we will satisfy him and keep you out of trouble." So they took the money and did as they were directed. And this story has been spread among the Jews to this day.

There have also been a few slight alterations to the stolen body theory to explain the empty tomb. For example, James Tabor, in his book *The Jesus Dynasty*, doesn't argue the disciples stole the body of Jesus at all. Rather, he argues that Jesus' body was "moved by someone and likely reburied in another location."[4] Atheist Richard Carrier has spouted in *The Plausibility of Death* the feasible idea that grave robbers were behind the stealing of Jesus' body. Carrier provides no real case study, just a weak argument that merely produces speculation, nothing more. Therefore, we will not address his argument, but only the stolen body theory.

Response

The stolen body and moved body theories fail for several reasons. First, the Jews faced an unexpected dilemma and had to figure out how to get in front of the resurrection narrative. Hence the notified remark by Matthew, "And this story has been spread among the Jews" (Matthew 28:15). The story was that the disciples stole the body; however, the last thing the Jewish leaders wanted were rumors of an empty tomb circulating around Jerusalem. The Jewish authorities wanted to squelch the public announcement that Jesus was resurrected. But why would the Jews pay off the Roman guards to say the tomb was indeed empty? Why concede to the disciples' reports? The best explanation is that the Jews knew the tomb was empty and had no body to exhume. William Lane Craig notes:

> Now what were unbelieving Jews saying in response to the disciples' proclamation that Jesus was risen? That these men were full of new wine? That Jesus' body still lay in the tomb in the garden? No. They were saying, "The disciples stole away the body." The Jewish authorities did not deny the empty tomb but instead entangled themselves in a hopeless series of absurdities trying to explain it away. In other words, the Jewish claim that the disciples had stolen the body presupposes that the body was missing.[5]

The Jews couldn't blame the Romans for taking the body, because neither group (Jews nor Romans) had an incentive to take the body (and if they did, they could have just exhumed the body to silence the disciples). However, the Jews put forth the story that the disciples (somehow) overcame the guards (who were placed there by Pilate [see Matthew 27:65–66]), pulled away a large stone, and successfully escaped with the dead body of Jesus.

Second, why on earth would the disciples fabricate a story like this? If they knew Jesus lied and died, then why would they abandon their Jewish roots, readily believe and spread a lie within their community, and give up their lives for a hoax? Liars don't make good martyrs.

For the sake of argument, let's assume (for a moment) that the disciples did steal Jesus' dead body from the tomb. How then did they defeat trained, armed Roman soldiers, move away a massive stone from the entrance of the tomb, and steal Jesus' lifeless body? Also, why would the disciples risk their lives by plotting and scheming a resurrection story when they all abandoned Jesus at the cross? Many of the disciples locked themselves away in fear of the Jewish leaders and the Romans. They knew they were next. The disciples were in no condition to overpower the Romans and steal the body. There is just no way untrained fighters (like the disciples) would have gotten past the Roman guards. And to say that the Roman guards fell asleep is highly unlikely. The Roman guards knew that if they failed their mission to guard Jesus' body, they would suffer the same death.

But let's pretend the Roman guards fell asleep. If so, how did they sleep through all the commotion of the disciples breaking into the tomb? Blaise Pascal provides a solid response to this ridiculous claim that the disciples were behind the embellished resurrected story:

> The apostles were either deceived or deceivers. Either supposition is difficult, for it is not possible to imagine that a man has risen from the dead. While Jesus was with them, he could sustain them; but afterwards, if he did not appear to them, who did make them act? The

hypothesis that the Apostles were knaves is quite absurd. Follow it out to the end, and imagine these twelve men meeting after Jesus' death and conspiring to say that he has risen from the dead. This means attacking all the powers that be. The human heart is singularly susceptible to fickleness, to change, to promises, to bribery. One of them had only to deny his story under these inducements, or still more because of possible imprisonment, tortures and death, and they would all have been lost. Follow that out.[6]

Taken together, this theory holds no weight that the disciples stole the body, concocted a wild story of a lowly carpenter who was cursed on the cross, claimed Him as a victorious, risen Savior, and successfully advanced this flimsy narrative into the greatest religion in history. Therefore, the conspiracy theory of a stolen body or that someone moved the body carries with it no real evidence to fit the facts.

Objection #3: Hallucination Theory

The Disciples Lost Their Minds

The final theory we will consider here is the delusional or hallucination theory. This position holds to the belief that perhaps these sightings of Jesus were nothing more than hallucinations. Considering Jesus' followers were so distraught over His death, they were delusional in thinking they saw Jesus when in fact they were only hallucinating. After some time, many became convinced that their hallucinations were visions and felt the need to share them with others. Then, before you know it, Christianity was born.

Response

First off, how's it even possible to have over five hundred witnesses all have the same delusional sightings of the post-resurrected Christ? Not to mention, why would they all bank on these "hallucinations" or "visions" of a resurrected Christ if they knew He was dead? They all knew He died on the cross, so there was hardly any reason to suspect to see Him postmortem.

Generally, it is people who were married who often say they saw their deceased loved ones, and those types of hallucinations don't appear consistently to different individuals. Furthermore, hallucinations are exactly that—they aren't real. The disciples were deeply emotional and traumatized, but that doesn't mean what they *thought* they witnessed was nothing more than hallucinations. Even if some shared what they believed to have been a vision of the post-resurrected Jesus, many would write it off because of their emotional state, not go out and start a worldwide religion in the very heart of Jerusalem.

C. S. Lewis, in his book *Miracles,* puts together a strong refutation to the hallucination theory. He writes:

> Any theory of hallucination breaks down on the fact (and if it is invention [rather than fact], it is the oddest invention that ever entered the mind of man) that on three separate occasions this hallucination was not immediately recognized as Jesus (Lk 24:13–31; Jn 20:15; 21:4). Even granting that God sent a holy hallucination to teach truths already widely believed without it, and far more easily taught by other methods, and certain to be completely obscured by this, might we not at least hope that he would get the face of the hallucination

right? Is he who made all faces such a bungler that he cannot even work up a recognizable likeness of the Man who was himself?[7]

And finally, the appearances of Jesus were something more. Many of the independent eyewitnesses reported having conversed, touched, ate, and walked with Jesus post-resurrection (see Matthew 28:9–10; Mark 16:1–8; Luke 24:13–16, 34; John 20:14–16, 26–28; Acts 9:3–5). To simply say that the disciples were under some sort of hallucination is plainly false based on the eyewitness reports.

Space doesn't permit us to delve into other alternate theories, but we believe providing you with the swoon theory, the stolen body theory, and the hallucination theory summarizes the best attempts to refute the resurrection. However, in so doing, based on our reasonable responses, these (nor any other natural theories) are plausible explanations to the resurrection. As we have shown, they offer up no real substantive arguments that bring in any new and hard-hitting facts.

As well, they don't do justice in providing credible explanations as to what is known to be true and accurate—for instance, the fact was that Jesus was buried, the tomb was identified, the tomb was found empty, and multiple eyewitnesses claimed to see Jesus post-resurrection. And finally, every natural explanation outside of what we know according to the Gospel accounts creates more questions than answers. Therefore, the natural objections to a risen Christ are more fanciful than real.

This leads us to the best explanation, which is that Jesus really did rise from the dead. To show that this is in fact true, we will give you an acronym—RISEN—that will help you remember key pieces of evidence for the resurrection.

Record of Jesus' death
Interment of Jesus
Significant appearances
Extraordinary conversions
New life and message

He Has RISEN

Record of Jesus' Death

The record of Jesus' death is important, because if we take the great drops of blood He suffered in the garden of Gethsemane (where His capillaries were bursting) and the thorns crushed on His head, to the brutal beatings and floggings from His shoulders to His lower thighs (ripping away muscle tissue and exposing organs), to the excruciating pain of being nailed to the cross for six hours (from nine in the morning to three in the afternoon), and then the final spear to His side, there's no possible way Jesus could have survived. What is surprising is how long Jesus did survive until He died.

In Luke 23:46, it states that Jesus gave up His spirit and died. As though that was not enough, a Roman soldier pierced Jesus' side with a spear, which alone would have been fatal. The spear struck the pericardium, the area around the heart, and the fact that blood and water came out was an indication that He had already suffered death.

Moreover, Pontius Pilate, before giving the body to Joseph to be buried, verified that Jesus was in fact dead. Mark 15:44–45 reads, "Pilate was surprised to hear that he should have already died. And summoning the centurion, he asked him whether he was already dead. And when he learned from the centurion that he was dead, he granted the corpse to Joseph." Thus, on all accounts, Jesus was dead.

Interment of Jesus

The burial of Jesus is one of the most established facts about what happened to Jesus after He was taken down from the cross. First, the burial story has well-attested, early, and independent sources. The accounts of Mark's Gospel (the first of the four Gospels written in the early 50s AD) contains eyewitness testimony within a few short years after the resurrection narrative. Additionally, according to 1 Corinthians 15:3–5, one of the earliest creeds, Paul writes, "For I delivered to you as of first importance what I also received: that Christ *died* for our sins in accordance with the Scriptures, that he was *buried*, that he was *raised* on the third day in accordance with the Scriptures, and that he *appeared* to Cephas, then to the twelve."

In his extensive book *Reasonable Faith*, Dr. Craig puts together the significance of this early creed quoted by Paul. He writes:

> Paul in 1 Corinthians 15:3–5 quotes an old Christian tradition that he had received from the earliest disciples. Paul probably received this tradition no later than his visit to Jerusalem in A.D. 36 (Gal. 1:18), if not earlier in Damascus. It thus goes back to within the first five years after Jesus' death. The tradition is a summary of the early Christian preaching and may have been used in Christian instruction.[8]

Second, a leading scholar on the resurrection of Jesus, Dr. Gary Habermas, investigated over 2,200 scholarly publications since 1975 involving the historical accounts of Jesus' resurrection. What he discovered was that over 75 percent of conservatives and liberals confirmed not only that Jesus was buried, but also that the tomb was indeed empty.

Third, no credible historian denies that Pilate verified the death of Jesus and authorized Joseph of Arimathea to lay Him in his tomb, that Joseph of Arimathea owned the tomb, that guards were placed there, and that the tomb was sealed by a large stone.

Fourth, the fact that Joseph of Arimathea placed Jesus in his own family burial site gives an identification that provides a location of where Jesus was buried. Joseph of Arimathea was an unlikely character at the time because he was a part of the Sanhedrin. Although he became a disciple prior to the death of Christ, the disciples wouldn't have mixed up a leader of the Sanhedrin with being the one in charge of embalming Jesus.

When putting together these (and other) historical facts, it's no wonder why A. T. Robinson (late professor at Cambridge University) emphasized that the burial of Jesus in the tomb is "one of the earliest and best-attested facts about Jesus."[9]

Significant Appearances

The fact that there were multiple eyewitnesses who claimed to see, converse with, and interact with the postmortem Jesus infers an empty tomb. Mary Magdalene was the first person to see the resurrected Christ. She and a few other women were the first to come upon Jesus' tomb and find it to be empty. This may seem incidental, but in those days, women as witnesses were not accepted. William Lane Craig explains:

Women occupied a low rung on the Jewish social ladder. This is evident in such rabbinic expressions as

"Sooner let the words of the law be burnt than delivered to women" and "Happy is he whose children are male, but woe to him whose children are female." The testimony of women was regarded as so worthless that they were not even permitted to serve as legal witnesses in a court of law. In light of these facts, how remarkable must it seem that it is women who are the discoverers of Jesus' empty tomb. Any later legend would certainly have made the male disciples to discover the empty tomb. The fact that women, whose testimony was worthless, rather than men, are the chief witnesses to the empty tomb is most plausibly accounted for by the fact that, like it or not, they were the discoverers of the empty tomb and the gospels accurately record this.[10]

To leverage credibility, the disciples wouldn't have picked women to be the initial witnesses of their elaborated story. Women were ineligible to be legal witnesses. Furthermore, upon the women's return from the tomb, they told the disciples that they had seen the resurrected Christ. In Luke 24:11, it says that "these words seemed to [the disciples] an idle tale, and they did not believe [the women]." This is hardly something to put into a made-up story. The only likely reason that the women are recorded as the first eyewitnesses and that the disciples initially disbelieved their report is because that's exactly what happened. The women and the disciples were telling the truth.

In 1 Corinthians 15:5–8, Paul gives a historical record of an early tradition that independently reports of people who saw the resurrected Christ: "[Jesus] appeared to *Cephas*, then to the *twelve*. Then he appeared to more than *five hundred brothers* at one time, most of whom are still alive, though some have fallen asleep. Then he appeared to *James*, then to all the *apostles*. Last of all, as to one untimely born, he appeared also to me."

Resurrection Appearances by H. L. Wilmington[11]

1. First appearance: to Mary Magdalene as she remained at the site of the tomb (see John 20:11–17).
2. Second appearance: to the other women who were also returning to the tomb (see Matthew 28:9–10).
3. Third appearance: to Peter (see Luke 24:34; 1 Corinthians 15:5).
4. Fourth appearance: to the disciples as they walked on the road to Emmaus (see Mark 16:12–13; Luke 24:13–31).
5. Fifth appearance: to the ten disciples (see Mark 16:14; Luke 24:36–51; John 20:19–23).
6. Sixth appearance: to the eleven disciples a week after His resurrection (see John 20:26–29).
7. Seventh appearance: to seven disciples by the Sea of Galilee (see John 21:1–23).
8. Eighth appearance: to five hundred others (see 1 Corinthians 15:6).
9. Ninth appearance: to James, the Lord's brother (see 1 Corinthians 15:7).
10. Tenth appearance: to the eleven disciples on the mountain in Galilee (see Matthew 28:16–20).
11. Eleventh appearance: at the time of the ascension (see Luke 24:44–53; Acts 1:3–9).
12. Twelfth appearance: to Stephen just prior to his martyrdom (see Acts 7:55–56).

13. Thirteenth appearance: to Paul on the road to Damascus (see Acts 9:3–6; 22:6–11; 26:13–18).
14. Fourteenth appearance: to Paul in Arabia (see Galatians 1:12–17).
15. Fifteenth appearance: to Paul in the temple (see Acts 9:26–27; 22:17–21).
16. Sixteenth appearance: to Paul while he was in prison in Caesarea (see Acts 23:11).
17. Seventeenth appearance: to the apostle John (see Revelation 1:12–20).

When we consider the number of substantial eyewitnesses to the postmortem Jesus, it's hard to deny the direct lines of evidence, especially the five hundred witnesses who saw Jesus at one time. Paul puts forth the challenge that, when in doubt, go out and question many of the five hundred witnesses who were still alive (though some had passed away) if his resurrection accounts seemed flawed. Dr. Charles Ryrie comments:

> All the appearances of the Lord after the resurrection are evidence that He did rise, and those appearances came at various times, to various people, and under various circumstances—all of which indicate that they were not staged (Jn 20:11–17; Mt 28:9–10; 1 Co 15:5; Lk 24:13–35, 36–43; Jn 20:26–29; 21:1–23; 1 Co 15:6). The sheer number of witnesses to the appearances of Christ after the resurrection makes it impossible to conceive of the story being fabricated by a few.[12]

Simon Greenleaf (1783–1853), the legendary lawyer and Harvard professor who wrote textbooks on legal evidence, came to believe in Christianity based on the overwhelming proof of the gospel witnesses. He concluded, "Copies which had been as universally received and acted upon as the Four Gospels, would have been received in evidence in any court of justice, without the slightest hesitation."[13]

Evaluating the multiple attestations of the post-resurrection appearances of Jesus Christ—from the women's eyewitness accounts, to Peter and John, to the other disciples, to Thomas (who doubted but then believed), to over five hundred people all at once—is proof positive that Jesus rose from the dead.

Extraordinary Conversions

The biblical account is filled with extraordinary conversions—people like Saul of Tarsus and James, the half-brother of Jesus, becoming believers, and some of the Jewish leaders who came to Christ. And then on the day of Pentecost we see over three thousand souls come to Christ (see Acts 2).

Paul the apostle and James (the half-brother of Jesus) are two of the most extraordinary conversions to Christianity. There is no other explanation than a resurrected Christ to convert James. We are told that he never believed Jesus was the Messiah during His entire ministry (see Mark 3:21, 31–35). But after the resurrection, James was in the upper room with the other disciples (see Acts 1:14), was the person the early church reported to (see Acts 12:17), was referred to as a "pillar" in the church (see Galatians 2:9), and later became the head of the Jerusalem church (see Acts 21:18). The only explanation for such an extraordinary conversion is an extraordinary event, like the resurrection.

Regarding Paul's conversion, Gary Habermas writes:

In contemporary critical studies, the apostle Paul is almost always thought to be the best witness among the

New Testament writers. A former opponent of this message, Paul clearly points out that the risen Jesus appeared personally to him. Paul makes this claim more than once (1 Cor. 9:1; 15:8; Gal. 1:16). We also have corroboration of Paul's testimony from another New Testament author, who retells the story three times (Acts 9:1–8; 22:3–11; 26:9–18). The data behind the fact of Paul's conversion from being an enemy of the church are recognized by all. But there needs to be a reason for this brilliant young scholar being convinced against his former beliefs and persecution of believers, as he explains (1 Cor. 15:9; Gal. 1:13–14; Phil. 3:4–7). Paul's reason is very clear: he was persuaded that he had seen the risen Lord. Therefore Paul was obviously an eyewitness to his experience.[14]

These are just some of the extraordinary conversions that took place after the death and resurrection of Jesus Christ. No doubt the disciples' transformations are hard proof that their faith was placed in a resurrected Savior. They went from denial and abandonment to an undeniable change of faith that gave them the courage to publicly proclaim Jesus Christ as Lord and Savior. So moving and compelling are the disciples' transformative experiences that even the most critical scholars affirm them to be historical.

New Life and Message

This is important because from the heart of Judaism we see Christianity spring forth. The disciples went from observing the Sabbath (Saturday) to worshiping together on Sunday. The early church implemented two ordinances that were fulfilled in Christ: baptism and communion. The early Christians were meeting in homes and leaving the synagogue, all the while preaching and teaching that Jesus Christ is Lord. Again, the only reasonable explanation for the disciples to radically alter their social structures was because of the risen Jesus. Gary Habermas writes:

> Jesus' resurrection was the *very center* of early Christian faith also indicates its reality, since, for this reason, it was repeatedly affirmed by believers and challenged by unbelievers. For example, Paul visited the Jerusalem apostles at least two or three times in order to make sure that his Gospel message was truthful. Indeed, there was no Christianity without this event (see 1 Cor. 15:14, 17). It was the church's central proclamation (see Acts 4:33). Unbelievers attacked this centerpiece of faith, but could not disprove the rock on which it was founded: Jesus' appearances.[15]

And Paul L. Maier concludes:

> If all the evidence is weighed carefully and fairly, it is indeed justifiable, according to the canons of historical research, to conclude that the tomb in which Jesus was buried was actually empty on the morning of the first Easter. And no shred of evidence has yet been discovered in literary sources, epigraphy, or archaeology that would disprove this statement.[16]

Do You Know Jesus?

Hopefully, we've shown you enough compelling evidence that Jesus did in fact rise from the dead. And if He did, what does that mean for you? Maybe you're a believer and you're needing more hope in your life. Maybe you are a skeptic. Maybe you're still searching. Maybe you're seeking. Maybe you are even praying for a sign from God, and you are waiting for that answer.

The truth is that we are not promised a life without pain. We're not promised a life without struggle. In fact, this is a fallen, broken world. There are a lot of tears and a lot of heartache, and our world is one where, sadly, there are oftentimes goodbyes. We live in a world where relationships break up, families dissipate, and loved ones die. But there is hope for those who believe in the promise of Jesus' resurrection. As a believer in Christ, we have hope for tomorrow. Not only are we forgiven in Christ, but we await the blessed reunion in heaven.

> We live in a world where relationships break up, families dissipate, and loved ones die. But there is hope for those who believe in the promise of Jesus' resurrection.

A profound verse in the Bible that encapsulates the value of the resurrection is Romans 8:11: "And if the Spirit of him who raised Jesus from the dead is living in you, he who raised Christ from the dead will also give life to your mortal bodies because of his Spirit who lives in you" (NIV). We see the same power in 1 Corinthians 6:14 when we are told, "And God raised the Lord and will also raise us up by his power." As a Christian, you have hope—not just in the here and now, but for eternity.

To those of you who have never trusted Christ as Savior: We want you to know that Jesus can and will forgive you of your sins if you let Him. You might be saying, "Yeah, Jason and Alex, you have no idea what kind of life I've lived. Why would Jesus want to forgive me?" In John 6:37, Christ says, "All that the Father gives me will come to me, and whoever comes to me I will never cast out." Jesus loves you—He died for your sins because He wants you to spend eternity with Him.

Jesus said in John 15:13, "Greater love has no one than this, that someone lay down his life for his friends." Well, guess what? Jesus loves you so much that He gave up His life so that you could have life in Him! There is no sin too great for Christ to forgive. In the Gospel of Luke, there's recorded an encounter that Jesus had with a woman whose "sins were many" (7:47), and yet her sins were forgiven. The Bible tells us that it's God's kindness, forbearance, and patience that leads us to repentance (see Romans 2:4–6).

After reading this book, hopefully you have concluded that Jesus Christ is the Son of God, and you are willing to surrender your life to Him—to ask Jesus to be Lord and Savior of your life. If so, you can pray to Jesus right now:

> Lord, I admit I'm a sinner, and I repent of my sin. I ask for you to forgive me of my sins. I believe you are the risen Son of God. I'm calling on your name, Jesus, to come into my life. I believe that you lived a sinless life, that you died on the cross for my sins and rose again on the third day. Thank you for loving me! Thank you for forgiving me! Thank you for giving me everlasting life with you in heaven. I give my life to you, and pray that from this day forward I will bring glory and honor to your name! In your name, I pray. Amen.

Jesus said in John 6:40, "For this is the will of my Father, that everyone who looks on the Son and believes in him should have eternal life, and I will raise him up on the last day." You can rest assured that if you sincerely (in faith) prayed this prayer, then we welcome you to the family of God. The Bible says, "To all who did receive him, who believed in his name, he gave the right to become children of God, who were born, not of blood nor of the will of the flesh nor of the will of man, but of God" (John 1:12–13).

The resurrection is more than just an event that occurred in history. It's what gives us life today and for all eternity! Because of the resurrection, we can overcome sin and live lives of hope, peace, and joy in the power of the Holy Spirit that raised Jesus from the dead.

CHAPTER 7

WHAT'S THE BEST WAY TO STUDY THE BIBLE?

I meditate on your precepts
and consider your ways.
I delight in your decrees;
I will not neglect your word.
—PSALM 119:15–16 NIV

In previous chapters, we talked about how the reading of the Bible is scarce among Christians today. It's gotten so bad that less than 20 percent of Christians read the Bible every day. We also examined the biblical evidence that shows why we can trust the Bible. In this chapter, we now turn our attention to the question, What is the best way to study the Bible?

Oh no. There's that word. *Study.*

You might be freaking out right now. Studying can be intimidating, especially when you're studying for a test. But relax. We are not here to quiz you on what you know. This is not a pass-or-fail chapter. What we want to do is give you the proper tools on how to study the Bible for your own personal enrichment. It is our desire that you enjoy reading and studying the Bible. More importantly, we want you to get as much out of the Word of God as you possibly can.

In 2 Timothy 2:15, Paul told Timothy, "Do your best to present yourself to God as one approved, a worker who has no need to be ashamed, rightly handling the word of truth." Just like Timothy, we too must devote our time and energy to learn how to "rightly handle" the Bible. Paul's challenge wasn't for Timothy to learn the Word whenever he felt like it; Paul wanted Timothy to not just know the Bible accurately, but to also faithfully live it and correctly teach it.

Preparing Your Heart

In my (Jason's) home, we have Psalm 19:14 on the wall going down the staircase of our house. It reads, "Let the words of my mouth and the meditation of my heart be acceptable in your sight, O LORD, my rock and my redeemer." The reason I put it there was so that my family would see it every morning when we come down the stairs to start our day. I am constantly encouraging my kids to start the day with that prayer. We don't know what we're going to say throughout the day and how we are going to act throughout the day. We may have a certain plan for the day, person to meet, or job to do, but whatever the day brings, we must pray that God's Word is reflected in our lives. However, if we want the Word to be evident in our lives, then we have to spend time in it.

I (Alex) remember a dear friend of mine telling me that Christian growth requires an investment. He would tell me, "Salvation is the same for everybody, but Christian growth is different for everybody." As a follower of Jesus Christ, we have to put some skin in the game. God could have downloaded His Word into our minds, but we're not a hard drive. We're not a machine. We're human beings with whom God wants a relationship.

> God has given us His Word so that we can be complete and lack nothing.

God has given us His Word so that we can be complete and lack nothing. Before we start unpacking how to study the Bible, we first want to give you four key disciplines to put in place before discussing methodology.

Start Your Study with Prayer

The Spirit of God wants the Word of God to be understood by the child of God. Many times before I begin to study the Bible, I (Alex) will pray through James 1:5, which says, "If any of you lacks wisdom, let him ask God, who gives generously to all without reproach, and it will be given him." So I'll say, "Lord, help me; give me wisdom today." Proverbs 1:7 promises us, "The fear of the LORD is the beginning of wisdom." God will honor the prayer I pray. If you come to the Word and say, "Lord, help me. I really want to get what you have to tell me, so Lord, help me understand it," God will honor that prayer. In Psalm 119:18, David prayed, "Open my eyes that I may behold wondrous things out of your law." That is a great prayer to pray. The key is to pray before you study the Bible.

The Discipline of Reverence

I (Jason) try to come to the Word of God reverently because it is holy. People gave their lives and were martyred, some facing death at the stake, all to get the Bible into the hands of the people in their own language. As the flames consumed his body, William Tyndale, who was responsible for translating the New

Testament into English, said, "Oh God, open the eyes of the King of England."[1] We need to understand that this is a holy book because its content is from God.

With reverence comes a righteous fear. As we spend time in the Bible, it reminds and convicts us that we are in the presence of a holy God. Reverence and fear go well beyond appreciating that we have the Bible. If you got a letter from the president of the United States, you wouldn't just toss it aside and say, "I'll get to this later." No, you would say, "Oh my goodness, the president wrote me!" Well, in the Bible, the God of the universe has written a message to you. We should approach it with reverence.

Receptiveness

Be open to hearing from God. When we have a set time with God, what we are saying is that we want to hear from Him. In Luke 8:15, Jesus said a receptive heart not only hears the Word of God but also cultivates it, so that it can bear much fruit: "As for that in the good soil, they are those who, hearing the word, hold it fast in an honest and good heart, and bear fruit with patience." And James tells us "to be quick to hear" (James 1:19). That's a receptive heart, a heart that is eager to hear and obey what God's Word says. When you open the Bible, pray that the power of God's Word opens your heart!

> Don't beat yourself up. God isn't looking for superstars; rather, He is looking for foot soldiers.

Consistency

Try not to be hot one day and cold the next. Be stable. Get into a routine and build a rhythm of when, where, and how you will study the Bible. Just remember: Don't beat yourself up. God isn't looking for superstars; rather, He is looking for foot soldiers. A faithful soldier of Christ is consistently learning and training himself or herself in the Word of God. Joshua 1:8 says, "This Book of the Law shall not depart from your mouth, but you shall meditate on it day and night, so that you may be careful to do according to all that is written in it. For then you will make your way prosperous, and then you will have good success."

True study and discipline comes with consistency. It is going to be difficult, and that is why the best way to study the Bible is to begin and end with obedience. Don't just read the Bible; read it, meditate on it, and study it. And as you do these, we encourage you to make an effort to disciple other Christians to do the same.

Why Study the Bible?

Let's start by examining three verses that show the value of the Bible and the consequences of not studying and applying it:

1. Psalm 119:11: "I have stored up your word in my heart, that I might not sin against you."

The consequence of this is that you will have more sin in your life if you don't "store up" God's Word in your heart.

2. Psalm 119:105: "Your word is a lamp unto my feet and a light to my path."

The consequence is that you will be led astray without the guidance of God's Word.

3. Luke 11:28: "Blessed rather are those who hear the word of God and keep it!"

The consequence of not listening to this verse is that you will not be blessed if you forsake God's Word.

Let's now turn our attention to three constructive reasons we should study the Bible: authority, conviction, and blessing.

1. Authority: What You Believe
   - The Bible is inspired by God (see 2 Timothy 3:16–17).
   - The Bible is infallible (trustworthy) (see Psalm 19:7).
   - The Bible is inerrant (without error) (see Proverbs 30:5–6).
   - The Bible is complete (see Revelation 22:18–19).
   - The Bible is authoritative (see Psalm 119:89).

2. Conviction: What You Receive
   - You will be sanctified in truth (see John 17:17).
   - You will be blessed (see Luke 11:28).
   - You will be victorious (see Ephesians 6:17).
   - You will grow in spiritual maturity (see 1 Peter 2:2).
   - You will receive power (see Romans 1:16).
   - You will attain guidance (see Psalm 119:105).

3. Blessing: What You Achieve
   - A growing faith (see John 6:68–69).
   - An obedient faith (see 1 John 2:5).
   - A strong faith (see Jude 3).
   - A prepared faith (see 2 Timothy 4:2).

Where Do I Start?

The truth is that most Christians have a *desire* to study the Bible; it's just that they lack the *drive* to do it. Let's now shift our attention to *how* we can go about learning God's Word for all it's worth.

Tip #1: Get the Basics Down

Before jumping right into studying the Bible, we highly recommend that you purchase *30 Days to Understanding the Bible* by Max Anders. This book will not only give you the *skeleton* of the Bible, but it also explains the Bible's key structure and lays out the Bible's parts in a way that makes sense. We also recommend these additional Bible resources:

- *Know Your Bible Illustrated: All Sixty-Six Books Explained and Applied* by Paul Kent
- *Bible Timeline Pamphlet* by Rose Publishing
- *How to Read the Bible for All Its Worth* by Gordon Fee and Douglas Stuart
- *Read the Bible for All Its Worth* by Dr. George Gutherie
- *Living by the Book* by Howard and William Hendricks
- *Holman Illustrated Bible Handbook* by HCSB
- *Navigating the Bible: The 5-Minute Guide to Understanding God's Word* by Christopher D. Hudson

Tip #2: Figure Out a Game Plan

Teams need a game plan. Corporations need a game plan. Couples need a game plan. Therefore, you need a game plan when it comes to studying the Bible. Here's some Bible reading plans that you can look over and decide on which one suits you the best:

- Read the Bible through in a year.
- Read the Old Testament in six months.
- Read the New Testament in three months.
- Read two Old Testament chapters, two New Testament chapters, one Psalm, and one Proverb each day.

- Inductive study of a particular book of the Bible (verse by verse).
- Topical studies and memorization.

We personally recommend that you start with something easy and gradually work yourself into a pattern that you can build upon. If you get behind, set some time aside to get caught up. But whatever you do, don't panic and quit! Stay on track and seek out additional accountability (if needed). Also, get yourself a good study Bible, Bible software, or a solid website that will help you better study and understand the Bible. This is an investment, but one that is worth every penny. Be sure to stick to a plan that keeps you focused and progressing in your reading every day.

Tip #3: Get Yourself Some Good Study Tools

This is usually the first thing Christians do when they choose to begin studying the Bible. They see a good study about a book of the Bible, purchase it, and then let it sit and collect dust. But if you follow the two tips above, then you will find yourself collecting and using the proper study tools that will help you flourish in your study of the Bible.

1. Books about the Bible and Bible Translations
   - *The Indestructible Book* by Ken Connolly
   - *The Word of God in English* by Leland Ryken
   - *Choosing a Bible* by Leland Ryken
   - *The Bible in Translation* by Bruce Metzger
   - *How We Got the Bible* by John Sailhamer
   - *A General Introduction to the Bible* by Norman Geisler and William Nix
   - *How to Choose a Translation for All Its Worth* by Gordon D. Fee and Mark L. Strauss

- *One Bible, Many Versions: Are All Translations Created Equal?* by Dave Brunn
- *How the Bible Came to Be,* edited by J. Daniel Hays and J. Scott Duvall
- *The Missing Gospels: Unearthing the Truth Behind Alternative Christianities* by Darrell Bock

2. Bible Difficulties
   - *Encyclopedia of Bible Difficulties* by Gleason Archer
   - *Hard Sayings of the Bible,* edited by Walter Kaiser, Peter Davids, F. F. Bruce, and Manfred Brauch
   - *When Critics Ask,* by Norman Geisler and Thomas Howe

3. Bible Interpretation
   - *Introduction to Biblical Interpretation,* by William Klein, Craig Blomberg, and Robert Hubbard Jr.
   - *Knowing Scripture,* by R. C. Sproul
   - *Exegetical Fallacies,* by D. A. Carson
   - *Scripture Twisting,* by James Sire
   - *How to Read the Bible for All Its Worth* by Gordon Fee and Douglas Stuart
   - *Out of Context: How to Avoid Misinterpreting the Bible* by Richard Schultz

Tip #4: Always Begin and End with Prayer

Always pray before you study the Bible. Ask God to open your heart to learn and obey His Word (see James 1:22–25). David prayed, "Search me, O God, and know my heart! Try me and know my thoughts! And see if there be any grievous way in me, and lead me in the way everlasting" (Psalm 139:23–24).

Also, make sure you journal your prayers (recorded prayers in the Bible: Moses' prayers [see Numbers 11:11–15; Psalm 90]; Hannah's prayer [see 1 Samuel 1]; the Lord's Prayer [see Matthew 6:9–13]; Paul's prayers [see Ephesians 3:16–19; Philippians 1:9–11; Colossians 1:9–14]).

Prayer is essential! We cannot stress this enough. There have been many times in our (Jason's and Alex's) lives when we have looked back on our prayers and been reminded of God's faithfulness as we studied the Word of God. So always make sure that you pray through what you study and make notes about it.

How Do I Study the Bible?[2]

Below are three key points to studying the Bible. The key is not to get too distracted and give up in the process.

Read to Observe: What's Going On?

The first step is *observation*. When reading the Bible, ask who, what, when, where, how, and why questions. The more insight you have of the *external* of the book, the deeper your understanding will be of the *internal* matters within the book. Thus, learning about the author, the date in which it was written, the background, and the historical setting will broaden your understanding of the *content* and *context* of the Bible.

Read to Interpret: What Does It Mean?

The next step is *interpretation*. An important rule to interpreting the Bible is context, context, context. David Cooper famously advises, "When the plain sense of Scripture makes common sense, seek no other sense; therefore, take every word at its primary, ordinary, usual, literal meaning unless the facts of the immediate context, studied in the light of related passages and axiomatic and fundamental truths, indicate clearly otherwise."[3]

The basic principle to hermeneutics (interpretation of the Bible) is to take a literal historical-grammatical interpretation to the Bible. Furthermore, Dr. John MacArthur mentions four primary "gaps" that need to be bridged when interpreting the Bible: (1) the language gap, (2) the culture gap, (3) the geographical gap, and (4) the historical gap.

- The language gap: Seek out the original meaning of the languages the Bible was written in (Hebrew, Aramaic, and Greek).
- The culture gap: Be sensitive to the culture and social structures of the time presented in the Bible.
- The geography gap: Allow geography to be a road map to help you understand the landscape and environment of the people in those times.
- The historical gap: Gain a historical perspective that will give you more appreciation of persons and events.

And finally, no matter what, always seek the Holy Spirit for illumination (see 1 Corinthians 2:10–11; 1 John 2:26–27).

Read to Apply: What Must I Do?

The last step is *application*. It's never enough to learn; you must also apply what you learn. Dr. Howard Hendricks offers three simple points to application: read to concentrate, record to remember, and reflect to apply.[4]

As we wrap up how to study the Bible, we want to leave you with a powerful prayer of Paul that demonstrates what we are to pray for as we study and live out the Word of God. In Colossians 1:9–14, Paul powerfully prayed:

For this reason, since the day we heard about you, we have not stopped praying for you. We continually ask God to fill you with the *knowledge of his will* through all the wisdom and understanding that the Spirit gives, so that you may *live a life worthy of the Lord* and please him in every way: *bearing fruit in every good work*, growing in the knowledge of God, being strengthened with all power according to his glorious might so that you may have great endurance and patience, and giving joyful thanks to the Father, who has qualified you to share in the inheritance of his holy people in the kingdom of light. For he has rescued us from the dominion of darkness and brought us into the kingdom of the Son he loves, in whom we have redemption, the forgiveness of sins. (NIV)

Revealed in this powerful prayer of Paul are three chief points: First, living the Word is to *know the will of God* (see Romans 12:1–2; Ephesians 5:15–17; 1 Thessalonians 4:1–3). Second, living the Word is to *walk worthy of God* (see Romans 6:4; Galatians 5:16; Ephesians 5:7). And third, living the Word is to *do the work of God* (see 1 Timothy 6:18; Titus 2:7). Therefore, it is only through the Word of God that we can know His will, walk worthy of the gospel, and complete the work God has put before us. And it is only by His Word that we can grow in our faith and become confident and passionate believers.

CHAPTER 8

SIX CHRISTIAN DUTIES TO KEEP YOU STRONG

We never grow closer to God when we just live life.
It takes deliberate pursuit and attentiveness.

—FRANCIS CHAN

We have all been called to various duties. Some duties we love to do, while others, not so much. When it comes to your job, there are certain duties that fall under your primary responsibilities, which are the duties you are expected and required to fulfill.

As I (Alex) am writing this, my wife and I are restoring an old house. As the homeowners, there are certain duties that fall on our shoulders and other duties that we can delegate to someone else. I've hired a general contractor, who helps me get the right guys for the right jobs. And the same goes for coaches and players, doctors and nurses, and our elected officials. Everyone has been given specific duties to fulfill.

But what about when it comes to our Christian walk? Are there duties given to us to fulfill? And if so, what happens if we choose not to do them? Before we get into our Christian duties, it's important to first clarify a few things.

First, the Bible makes it perfectly clear that there is nothing we can do to *earn* salvation on our own merit. Ephesians 2:8–9 reads, "For by grace you have been saved through faith. And this is not your own doing; it is the gift of God, not a result of works, so that no one may boast." Salvation is a free gift; it cannot be earned. God's grace (unmerited favor) isn't given because of what we have done; rather, it is given because of God's great love for us. God justifies us when we place our faith in the finished work of Christ. When we talk about fulfilling certain duties as a Christian, that's not to say these are things we must do to attain salvation. We don't keep adding good works in our lives to gain acceptance from God.

On the other hand, there is more pervasive thinking among Christians that says, "Well, if we're not saved by good works, then we don't really need to do anything at all." This is also wrong. Although we are not saved by good works, the Bible does say we are saved *for* good works. Paul writes in Ephesians 2:10, "For we are his workmanship, created in Christ Jesus *for good works*, which God prepared beforehand, that we should walk in them." Also in Titus 2:14, Paul writes, "Who gave himself for us to redeem us from all lawlessness and to purify for himself a people for his own possession who are *zealous for good works.*"

> It's easy to switch to autopilot in our Christian walk. We can sometimes get into a rut or get so accustomed to mundane prayers and going to church every Sunday that we neglect our responsibility to grow a stronger faith.

These good works that we as Christians are called to fulfill is what we want to discuss in this chapter. It's easy to switch to autopilot in our Christian walk. We can sometimes get into a rut or get so accustomed to mundane prayers and going to church every Sunday that we neglect our responsibility to grow a stronger faith. Christian growth, maturing in Christ, and becoming everything that the Lord intends us to be requires us to take part in the growth process. You might have a great pastor, attend a good church, or may have some spiritual mentors. These can certainly help you grow in your faith, but they can't do it for you. *Christian growth requires ownership. The more you own your faith and exercise it, the stronger your faith will be.* We have a call to take responsibility and grow in our faith to impact the lives of others.

Duty #1: Pray with Power

Jesus said the spirit is willing but the flesh is weak when it comes to prayer (see Matthew 26:41). We are each in the process of sanctification as we're living out our Christian life in this fallen world. There are struggles. We may have a desire, but we're not always dedicated or devoted to it. People say, "I have a desire; I want to go do missions, and I want to go serve." But we need to stop all that and learn how to pray with power.

We are to love God with all our heart, mind, and soul (see Matthew 22:37), so when we love to talk with God, it will strengthen our relationship with Him, which will strengthen our prayer life. This is something that everyone, no matter what stage in the sanctification process, is going to go through in this fallen world. We all can be praying more, praying with thanksgiving, and praying without ceasing, as the Bible says we are to do.

When I (Jason) was a boy, my dad took me to an all-night prayer gathering. The man leading the prayer group was a mighty prayer warrior. I can still hear his prayers. Man, were his prayers powerful. He had such faith and intimacy with God. Even though I was barely a teen at the time, I remember praying and asking God to give me that kind of power in prayer.

In Luke 18:1, Jesus said that we are to "always pray and not lose heart." Think about all the times you've prayed about something and nothing seemed to happen. How does that make you feel? When we pray and nothing seems to happen, it can get depressing, especially when it feels like God is nowhere to be found. Like Jesus said, we must not give up when we pray. We are not to doubt, grow weary, or give up on prayer. Billy Graham liked to say, "Pray harder when it's hardest to pray."

We should always pray. No matter the circumstance, we need to take it before the Lord. It's not our job to question God, but it is our job to earnestly pray to Him for answers. In Matthew 7:7–8, Jesus said, "Ask, and it will be given to you; seek, and you will find; knock, and it will be opened to you. For everyone who asks receives, and the one who seeks finds, and to the one who knocks it will be opened." Jesus commands us to keep on asking, seeking, and knocking with confidence, because our heavenly Father delights in giving us good gifts (see James 1:17).

This requires faith: "And without faith it is impossible to please him, for whoever would draw near to God must believe that he exists and that he rewards those who seek him" (Hebrews 11:6).

For everyone who asks receives, and the one who seeks finds, and to the one who knocks it will be opened. What father among you, if his son asks for a fish, will instead of a fish give him a serpent; or if he asks for an egg, will give him a scorpion? If you then, who are evil, know how to give good gifts to your children, how much more will the heavenly Father give the Holy Spirit to those who ask him! (Luke 11:10–13)

Therefore I tell you, whatever you ask in prayer, believe that you have received it, and it will be yours. (Mark 11:24)

Until now you have asked nothing in my name. Ask, and you will receive, that your joy may be full. (John 16:24)

You do not have, because you do not ask. (James 4:2)

We believe that God is eager and ready to give big-time answers to your prayers, but you need to come in a spirit of humility and with faith. And when you do so, you will start seeing what the power of prayer can do.

Duty #2: Hear from God

If something is truly from God, it will never contradict the Word of God. God will never direct you to do something that goes against His Word. Jeremiah 33:3 says, "Call to Me, and I will answer you, and show you great and mighty things that you do not know" (NKJV). God speaks to us in many ways, but primarily, and this is where we need to keep our ear attuned, He speaks through Scripture. That's the starting part. When you're praying about something specific, use the Scriptures as a guiding post. If you are wrestling with worry, unforgiveness, or what you should do about a job, the best thing to do is to look at what the Bible says about worry, forgiveness, and decision making.

Another thing we (Jason and Alex) often do is trace back to many of the recorded prayers and evaluate why David (for instance) prayed what he did in Psalm 86. Or why Hannah was so emotional in her prayer recorded in 1 Samuel 1. This gives us insight into their situations, but most importantly, it reminds us of the faithfulness of God as He responded to and answered their prayers. If God heard their prayers and spoke to them, then why can't He do the same for us?

This kind of faith and intimacy with God will open up a whole different relationship with Him. This is not the status-quo relationship. This is the one, we believe, God wants us to have with Him. He wants to speak to you, and share with you so many things, if you're willing to listen.

In his classic book *Hearing God: Developing a Conversational Relationship with God*, Dallas Willard writes:

> In our attempts to understand how God speaks to us and guides us, we must above all hold on to the fact that this is to be sought *only as a part of a certain kind of life*, a life of loving fellowship with the King and his other subjects within the kingdom of the heavens. We must never forget that God's speaking to us, however we experience it in our initial encounter, is intended to develop into an intelligent, freely cooperative relationship between mature people who love each other with the richness of genuine *agape* love. We must therefore make it our primary goal not just to hear the voice of God but to be mature people in a loving relationship with him. Only in this way will we hear him rightly.[1]

Something I (Jason) often do is sit and silently wait to hear from God. Just this morning I spent time on my knees silently waiting to hear from God. There were many times I began to shout praises to Him for who He is; a Scripture would come to mind, and I would read it, and then return to silence as I anticipated to hear the voice of God. I love being quiet in God's presence. There is so much peace, and it helps keep my focus on Him, rather than only on my requests.

You too can have confidence that you can hear the voice of God. Paul writes, "For all who are led by the Spirit of God are sons of God" (Romans 8:14). As you seek Him in prayer, you will be able to discern the voice of God as you are filled with and led by the Holy Spirit (see Ephesians 6:18). But again, this will only come if you make the investment to go deeper with God.

Duty #3: Know and Share What You Believe

Why is knowing and sharing what you believe important in the context of the Christian life? It's important because the Word of God commands us to know what we believe and the reasons we believe it. The Bible says that we are to study to show ourselves approved (see 2 Timothy 2:15), to "always [be] prepared to make a defense" (1 Peter 3:15), and to earnestly contend for the faith (see Jude 3). In addition, when it came to studying the Word of God and advancing in knowledge of the Christian faith, Paul wrote to Timothy: "Devote yourself to the public reading of Scripture, to exhortation, to teaching" (1 Timothy 5:13). As he does this, he is to continue to "practice and immerse himself" as he progresses in his spiritual abilities.

The Christian life is not to be lived half-heartedly. And yet, sadly, so many Christians spend more bandwidth thinking about where they're going to spend a week's vacation than they do thinking about what they believe.

Culturally speaking, we live in a world where dozens of belief systems are competing for the hearts and minds of people. This makes it critical that Christians develop a strong biblical worldview. It is important that Christians all over the world are gaining a rich theological understanding of what Christianity says about the nature of God, the origin of life, human identity, the incarnation, salvation, the church, and eternity; and that Christians are able to engage the culture with the gospel of Jesus in a spirit of love and truth, and to not back down.

Charles Colson and Nancy Pearcey stressed the importance of Christians having a strong biblical worldview in their book *How Now Shall We Live?* They write, "Understanding Christianity as a total life system is absolutely essential, for two reasons. First, it enables us to make sense of the world we live in and thus order our lives more rationally. Second, it enables us to understand forces hostile to our faith, equipping us to evangelize and to defend Christian truth as God's instruments for transforming culture."[2]

Prior to leaving earth, Jesus gave the commandment to "go and make disciples of all nations" (Matthew 28:19; see also Mark 16:15). This is known as the Great Commission. However, if we really don't know what it is we believe, then chances are we won't share our faith with others. Or to put it another way, *if our faith is not a real investment, then neither will we invest the time to lead people to faith.*

As you reflect on the challenge given directly by the verses provided above to study and to defend what you believe, hopefully you will deeply immerse yourself into building up a robust biblical worldview. If this is something you are already doing, we commend you and pray that you will continue to sharpen your faith, as well as look for the opportunity to teach others.[3]

Duty #4: Love Others

Loving others is the second greatest commandment given by God. Matthew 22:39 says that "you shall love your neighbor as yourself." And Jesus says in John 13:34–35, "A new commandment I give to you, that you love one another: just as I have loved you, you also are to love one another. By this all people will know that you are my disciples, if you have love for one another." Love is central to fellowship and to the church, as well as to exercising our spiritual gifts. Paul made it abundantly clear in 1 Corinthians 13:3 that without love we are nothing.

We who have been the recipients of great love should love all people.

Biblically speaking, love seeks the highest good of another. The lack of love and an increasing number of broken, fragmented relationships have destroyed churches and families. We, of all people, who have been forgiven should know how to forgive. We who have been the recipients of great love should love all people. Notice the responsibility given to all believers when it comes to demonstrating love:

Love one another with brotherly affection. Outdo one another in showing honor. (Romans 12:10)

Above all, keep loving one another earnestly, since love covers a multitude of sins. (1 Peter 4:8)

Beloved, let us love one another, for love is from God, and whoever loves has been born of God and knows God. (1 John 4:7)

Simply put, if we love God, we will love one another too. And the more we love others, the less we will sin against them. When we choose to love others, we will find ourselves forgiving more (see Colossians 3:13), accepting more (see Romans 15:7), and serving more (see Galatians 5:13).

Duty #5: Be a Good Steward

Are you a giver, or do you have a hard time giving to others? Jesus said, "One who is faithful in a very little is also faithful in much, and one who is dishonest in a very little is also dishonest in much. If then you have not been faithful in the unrighteous wealth, who will entrust to you the true riches?" (Luke 16:10–11). The bottom line is that where your treasure is, there your heart will be also (see Matthew 6:21). If you hold on to everything on earth, then you're not investing much in heaven. Randy Alcorn, a true steward of God, put it like this: "If you handle [God's] money faithfully, Christ will give you true riches—eternal ones. By clinging to what isn't ours, we forgo the opportunity to be granted ownership in heaven. But by generously distributing God's property on earth, we will become property owners in heaven!"[4] This is a choice only you can make.

If you know Jesus Christ as your Lord and Savior, then you have an inheritance. But the Bible also talks about storing up treasures in heaven, which takes hard work and resourcefulness. In the book of Philippians, Paul speaks of an eternal "credit" or "account," which seems to imply that God keeps a record of all the heavenly deposits we make. No doubt we can waste our resources, much like the prodigal son did (see Luke 15:11–13), and blow our chances at being a good steward of what God has given us.

The brilliant author and speaker, Ken Boa, gives a wealth of insight about stewardship:

> Biblical stewardship touches every area of our lives. It requires a basic commitment to present ourselves completely to God as his servants, with no strings attached. The real issue of stewardship is whether we are administrating our affairs and possessions as if they are ours or as if they are God's. Our lives are shaped by the decisions we make, and there is no greater choice offered to us than surrender to the one who created us and knows us better than we know ourselves. The ultimate question, then, is this: Am I the lord of my life, or is Christ the Lord of my life? We will either labor under the illusion that we can control our own lives, or we will submit to the reign and rule of God. This is the difference between the great I will and the great Thy will. Whether we realize it or not, we face this decision many times in the course of each day. Our answer to this question will determine how we manage the time, abilities, money, truth and relationships God has placed under our care. A wise steward will treat things according to their true value, treasure the things God declares to be important and hold with a loose grip the things that God says will not matter in the end.[5]

As a steward of God, you are to be found faithful (see 1 Corinthians 4:2) in your service to others (see Matthew 25:20–21) as you exercise your spiritual gifts for the glory of God (see 1 Peter 4:10). So the question you need to ask yourself is, What does my eternal bank account look like?

Duty #6: Persevere

We've placed this final duty at the end because without perseverance none of the other duties will ever be accomplished. In essence, the Christian is not a quitter. We are constantly being reminded in the Bible to be strong and to not lose heart. Paul told the church to not grow weary while doing good (see Galatians 6:9). Why did he say this? Because it's in our nature to quit, to want to give up. But let us be reminded that we are not our own. We belong to God, and He has given us His Spirit who dwells within us (see 1 Corinthians 6:19–20).

When things get tough and you feel like giving up, take comfort in the fact that He who is in you is greater than he who is in the world (see 1 John 4:4). Paul told the church in Galatia, "And let us not grow weary of doing good, for in due season we will reap, if we do not give up" (Galatians 6:9)—no matter the challenges, no matter the trials, no matter the problems. God is faithful. He will not abandon us or leave us to figure life out on our own. Jesus overcame sin and death, and He is preparing a place for us. At any given time, He will return to get His bride.

Keep on keeping on. Though the darkness may come and the feelings of despair creep in, hold fast to the promise that you are a warrior for Christ. The battle is not over. Keep fighting the good fight of faith. Keep standing strong. God will give you the strength needed to persevere through whatever you are facing (see Colossians 1:9–14). The great C. S. Lewis remarked, "God knows our situation; He will not judge us as if we had no difficulties to overcome. What matters is the sincerity and perseverance of our will to overcome them."[6]

There are certainly more duties mentioned in the Bible, but for our purposes here, we wanted to list a few to help you grow strong in your faith. Remember that these duties are yours to prosper in. God will bring people along to help you in various ways, but, of course, it's your sole duty to make sure they are not neglected in your life.

If you want to stand strong in your faith and grow confident and passionate in your relationship with Jesus, then don't neglect these duties. These six duties are vital to a strong and robust faith.

NOTES

Chapter 1: When in Doubt

1 For information about Summit Ministries, check out www.summit.org.

2 Timothy Keller, *The Reason for God: Belief in an Age of Skepticism* (New York: Riverhead, 2009), xvi–vii.

3 Dr. Gary Habermas, "Identifying Doubt," *John Ankerberg Show*, May 10, 2016, accessed February 28, 2017, https://www.jashow.org/articles/christian-living/doubt-christian-living/dealing-with-doubt/identifying-doubt.

4 Dr. Gary Habermas, "The Thomas Factor: Using Your Doubts to Draw Closer to God," *Bethinking.org*, accessed February 2, 2017, http://www.bethinking.org/truth/the-thomas-factor-using-your-doubts-to-draw-closer-to-god/6-emotional-doubt.

5 C. S. Lewis, *The Screwtape Letters* (New York: Harper, 2001), 148.

6 C. S. Lewis, *Mere Christianity* (New York: Macmillan Publishing, 1952), 123–124.

7 Os Guinness, *In Two Minds: The Dilemma of Doubt and How to Resolve It* (Downers Grove: InterVarsity Press, 1976), 33.

Chapter 2: How to Be Fearless in the Midst of Fear

1 Billy Graham, "Wit & Wisdom—Promises—The Billy Graham Library Blog," *The Billy Graham Library*, July 17, 2015, accessed February 28, 2017, https://billygrahamlibrary.org/wit-wisdom-promises.

2 Burk Parsons, "The Object of Our Faith," *Ligonier Ministries*, accessed February 10, 2017, http://www.ligonier.org/learn/articles/object-our-faith.

3 Gary R. Collins, *Christian Counseling: A Comprehensive Guide* (Dallas: Word Publishing, 1988), 66.

Chapter 3: Living Beyond Yourself: The Role of the Holy Spirit in the Believer's Life

1 Billy Graham, *The Holy Spirit: Activating God's Power in Your Life* (Dallas: Word Publishing, 1988), 14.

2 Norman L. Geisler and Jason Jimenez, *The Bible's Answers to 100 of Life's Biggest Questions* (Grand Rapids, MI: Baker Publishing Group, 2015), Kindle locations 1563–1572.

3 Ron Rhodes, "The Holy Spirit: A Deposit of What Is to Come," *5-Minute Apologetics for Today: 365 Quick Answers to Key Questions* (Eugene, OR: Harvest House, 2010), 217.

4 Edmund Clowney, "The Holy Spirit as Seal and Pledge," *Ligonier Ministries*, accessed February 13, 2017, http://www.ligonier.org/learn/articles/the-holy-spirit-as-seal-and-pledge.

5 Bill Bright, *How You Can Be Filled with the Holy Spirit* (Orlando, FL: NewLife Publications, 1998), 31.

6 Roy B. Zuck, *The Speaker's Quote Book: Over 5,000 Illustrations and Quotations for All Occasions* (Grand Rapids, MI: Kregel Academic & Professional, 2009), 256.

Chapter 4: The Most Neglected Thing in the World: The Bible

1 "State of the Bible 2016," *American Bible Society*, March 28, 2017.

2 Woodrow Kroll, "The New America and the New Bible Illiteracy," June 27, 2007, *WorldwiewWeekend*, accessed March 24, 2017, http://www.worldviewweekend.com/news/article/new-america-and-new-bible-illiteracy.

3 John Pavlovitz, "Church, Stop Hiring Preachers and Performers to Be Your Pastors," May 12, 2015, accessed February 14, 2017, http://johnpavlovitz.com/2015/09/07/church-stop-hiring-preachers-and-performers-to-be-your-pastors.

4 "Here's What Happens When Churches Don't Regularly Teach from the Bible," *Faithwire*, November 22, 2016, accessed February 14, 2017, http://www.faithwire.com/2016/11/22/heres-what-happens-to-churches-that-ignore-the-bible/.

5 Stephen Nichols, "The Baseball Evangelist," *The Baseball Evangelist | 5 Minutes in Church History*, June 22, 2016, http://5minutesinchurchhistory.com/the-baseball-evangelist/.

6 Søren Kierkegaard and Charles E. Moore, *Provocations: Spiritual Writings* (Walden, NY: Plough House, 2014), 201.

7 George Mueller, as cited by Henry H. Halley, "The Habit of Bible Reading," *Halley's Bible Handbook* (Grand Rapids, MI: Zondervan, 2014), 807.

8 George H. Guthrie, "How to Read and Study the Bible," *Holman Illustrated Bible Handbook* (Nashville, TN: Holman Bible, 2012), 3.

9 Ibid.

Chapter 5: How Can I Know the Bible Is True?

1 William F. Albright, as cited by Josh McDowell and Don Stewart, *Answers to Tough Questions: About the Christian Faith* (Bletchley: Authentic Media, 2006), 3.

2 Norman L. Geisler and Ronald M. Brooks, *When Skeptics Ask* (Wheaton, IL: Victor Books, 1990), 146.

3 Benjamin B. Warfield, as cited by Robert Saucy, *Scripture: Its Power, Authority, and Relevance* (Nashville: Word Publishing, 2001), 134.

4 Norman L. Geisler and William E. Nix, *From God to Us: How We Got Our Bible*, revised and expanded ed. (Chicago, IL: Moody Publishers, 1974), 92.

5 Ibid., 247.

6 For further study, read the chapter "The Bible is Scientifically Accurate" in *Examine the Evidence: Exploring the Case for Christianity*, by Ralph Muncaster.

7 Here are some additional resources that give more evidence on why you can trust the Bible: *From God to Us*, by Geisler and Nix; *The New Testament Documents: Are They Reliable?*, by F. F. Bruce; and *How We Got the Bible: A Visual Journey*, Zondervan Visual Reference Series, by Clinton Arnold.

Chapter 6: The Crux of History: Did Jesus Rise from the Dead?

1 Michael Green, *Man Alive!* (Downer Groves, IL: InterVarsity Press, 1968), 61.

2 William Lane Craig, *Knowing the Truth About the Resurrection* (Ann Arbor: MI, Servant, 1988), 116–17.

3 Marcus J. Borg and N. T. Wright, *The Meaning of Jesus: Two Visions* (San Francisco: Harper, 1998), 129–31.

4 James D. Tabor, *The Jesus Dynasty: The Hidden History of Jesus, His Royal Family, and the Birth of Christianity* (New York: Simon & Schuster, 2007), 234.

5 William Lane Craig, *On Guard: Defending Your Faith with Reason and Precision* (Colorado Springs, CO: David C. Cook, 2010), 214.

6 Blaise Pascal, *Pensees*, 800, 801.

7 C. S. Lewis, *Miracles: How God Intervenes in Nature and Human Affairs* (New York: Collier, 1978), 147–48.

8   William Lane Craig, *Reasonable Faith: Christian Truth and Apologetics* (Wheaton, IL: Crossway Books, 2008), 362.

9   Ibid., 364.

10 William Lane Craig, "Jesus' Resurrection | Reasonable Faith," *ReasonableFaith.org*, accessed February 24, 2017, http://www.reasonablefaith.org/jesus-resurrection.

11 H. L. Willmington, *Willmington's Book of Bible Lists* (Wheaton, IL: Tyndale, 1987), 168–69.

12 Charles Caldwell Ryrie, *A Survey of Bible Doctrine* (Chicago, IL: Moody Press, 1972).

13 Norman L. Geisler, "Resurrection of Christ," *Baker Encyclopedia of Christian Apologetics*, Baker Reference Library (Grand Rapids, MI: Baker Books, 1999), 649. See also *Testimony of the Evangelists*, by Simon Greenleaf.

14 Gary Habermas, "The Case for Christ's Resurrection," *To Everyone an Answer: A Case for the Christian World View*, ed. Francis J. Beckwith, William Lane Craig, and J. P. Moreland (Downers Grove, IL: InterVarsity Press, 2004), 182.

15 Gary Habermas, "The Resurrection Appearances of Jesus," *NAMB*, accessed February 27, 2017, https://www.namb.net/apologetics/the-resurrection-appearances-of-jesus.

16 Paul Barnett, *Is the New Testament Reliable?* (Downers Grove, IL: InterVarsity, 2003), 133.

Chapter 7: What's the Best Way to Study the Bible?

1   Michael McCormack, "Tyndale's Burning," *Killing the Bible*, accessed March 29, 2017, http://killingthebible.com/persecution-stories/tyndales-burning/.

2   Some of this material is taken from *Bible's Answers to 100 of Life's Biggest Questions*, by Geisler and Jimenez, 61–63.

3   Ed Hindson and Elmer Towns, *Illustrated Bible Survey: An Introduction* (Nashville: Broadman & Holman, 2017), 14.

4   Tim Newcomb, "Howard Hendricks' 4 Bible Study Steps," *Bible Study Magazine*, September 9, 2016, accessed March 29, 2017, http://www.biblestudymagazine.com/bible-study-magazine-blog/2016/7/27/howard-hendricks-4-bible-study-steps.

Chapter 8: Six Christian Duties to Keep You Strong

1 Dallas Willard, *Hearing God: Developing a Conversational Relationship with God* (Downers Grove, IL: InterVarsity, 1999), 31.

2 Charles W. Colson and Nancy Pearcey, *How Now Shall We Live?* (Wheaton, IL: Tyndale House, 1999), 16.

3 Here are some apologetic resources: *The Bible's Answers to 100 of Life's Biggest Questions*, by Geisler and Jimenez; *Stand: Core Truths You Must Know for An Unshakeable Faith*, by Alex McFarland; *I Don't Have Enough Faith to Be an Atheist*, with study guide, by Norman Geisler, Frank Turek, and Jason Jimenez; *The 10 Most Common Objections to Christianity*, by Alex McFarland.

4 Randy Alcorn, *Treasure Principle: Unlocking the Secret of Joyful Giving* (Colorado Springs, CO: Multnomah, 2008), 40.

5 Ken Boa, "Stewardship," *Bible.org*, November 2, 2005, accessed February 22, 2017, https://bible.org/seriespage/32-stewardship.

6 C. S. Lewis, *Mere Christianity* (New York: HarperOne, 2012), 99.

ABOUT THE AUTHORS

Jason Jimenez is the founder of Stand Strong Ministries. He is a pastor, apologist, and national speaker. In his extensive ministry career, Jason has spent a great deal of time investing in marriages, serving families, and helping churches have greater impact in their communities. Jason is the author of *The Raging War of Ideas: How to Take Back Our Faith, Family, and Country*, *The Bible's Answers to 100 of Life's Biggest Questions*, and *Abandoned Faith: Why Millennials Are Walking Away and How You Can Lead Them Home* (a Focus on the Family project). Jason and his wife live in Charlotte, North Carolina, with their four beautiful children. For more information, check out www.standstrongministries.org.

Alex McFarland is a speaker, writer, and advocate for apologetics, having preached in over fifteen hundred different churches throughout North America and internationally. He has been featured at conferences such as The Billy Graham School of Evangelism, The Big Dig˚ from Focus on the Family, and Josh McDowell's True Foundations events. He attended the University of North Carolina at Greensboro, and earned a master's degree in Christian thought and apologetics from Liberty University. He was awarded an honorary Doctor of Divinity degree by Southern Evangelical Seminary in 2006. He is married to Angie, who is the godly and supportive wife who has played a tremendous role in all that the Lord has called Alex to do. They have been married since 1988 and currently live in North Carolina.